# Voyage of the GIN PAHIT

Also by James Barclay:
A Stroll Through Borneo 1980
Travelling Hopefully 1987

# Voyage of the Gin Pahit
## Searching the Nusa Tenggara Islands in Indonesia from August to November 1980.

By James Barclay

# Contents

# *List of Illustrations:*

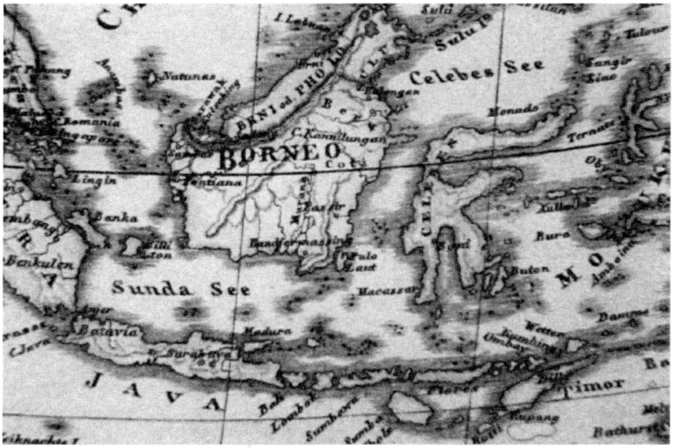


Bali at the middle bottom, and Wetter to the east of Bali, was the extent of the Gin Pahit's voyaging.

There were three trips between August and November 1980 with the common aim of finding a suitable home for the thousands of Vietnamese refugee 'boat people' who were leaving Vietnam in search of a better life.

The first consisted of Harry Fane, Mark Shand, myself, Made Monoh and John Roben sailing from Bali to Komodo Island.

The second was myself travelling mostly overland in the islands.

The third was myself and John Roben setting off from Bali in the Gin Pahit, John Roben leaving in Reo Bay, Flores, then sailing myself to Kampong Wuring near Maumere, Flores, and picking up a new crewman called Ewang and sailing to Wetar island and back to his kampong. Then sailing back from his kampong to Bali on my own.

This account is being published 30 years later, and owes much to computer technology - an unknown in 1980. Indeed to make a telephone call from Bali meant queuing up at the telecom office, often for about 20 hours, to take a turn on the only public international line. Many of the trials and tribulations were borne from being unable to communicate. If we could have fast forwarded and seen a world full of mobile telephones we would have jeered at a generation not knowing their luck.

# Chapter 1

## Preparing The Boat

Since the end of the Vietnam War the Vietnamese have been seeking to leave their newly united country. At times this exodus has reached vast numbers with a wide variety of local craft heading away from the Vietnam coastline intending to land anywhere where they could be processed and sent on to the West. As the numbers increased so the debate intensified as to what to do with them. It was reminiscent of the Jewish boat people from Europe trying to land in Palestine during the 1930s. Arguments revolved around whether these Vietnamese were genuine political refugees or economic migrants seeking a more prosperous home. Asian nations neighbouring Vietnam were almost all hostile to the boat people and in some cases, notably in Malaysia, hundreds if not thousands of refugees drowned within sight of a shore when their leaking overloaded boats were either pushed or towed back out to sea by local police. Public opinion in the west was divided as to who was responsible and what should be done. Almost everyone agreed that America should foot the main cost of solving the problem. Most people also felt that the Asian nations should take more responsibility for this Asian problem, however it was caused in the first place.

While passing through Singapore I met an official from the United Nations High Commission for Refugees and said to her, "Why are you sending Vietnamese boat people to overcrowded urban areas in the climatically, culturally and linguistically unsuitable West? There are thousands of islands in Indonesia for example and I am sure that one or two could serve either as a temporary camp for processing them into new homes in Asia or as a permanent home for them, such as the Banabans in Fiji."

She responded with an air of patient restraint by saying "I bet you that for however long you search through that enormous Indonesian archipelago, you would not find a single island that could be used for relocation purposes."

I decided to take her up on her challenge and said, "I will go to Indonesia in a month's time and start the search. Would you be interested in what I find?"

"Yes I would, please get in touch when you get back. Here is

my card", and she handed me a heavily embossed business card with a long name and job title.

This challenge fitted in with a tentative plan that I already had to visit Komodo island, home of the Komodo dragon, with two English friends, Mark and Harry, who owned a house in Bali. They had already made a start by arranging to buy a local Balinese boat, have it converted, and employ the former Balinese owner, Made Monoh, and his nephew, John, to act as captain and crew.

Getting to Komodo island, and any of the other islands in the Nusa Tengara group, east of Bali, involved travelling by local craft, and as none of us had much experience in any sort of a boat we decided to enrol in two courses in England involving engine maintenance and theoretical work. 'Rodge' Naldrett taught us all he knew about the innards of a diesel engine through diagrams and classroom work, and gave us practical tuition on an outboard engine 'poodling round' Chichester harbour.

On the sailing side we were fortunate to get enrolled on an intensive course with Denise St Aubyn Hubbard, the only female captain in the British navy and a veteran of the single-handed transatlantic race, who operated from Bosham. Most of what we were cramming was relevant to Western style boats and UK waters, but it at least gave us the necessary confidence to set off.

I felt more relaxed about any overland travel, because I had already done some jungle bashing through the Indonesian province of Kalimantan in Borneo, and the Nusa Tengara islands were generally less forested.

Maps, guide books, and charts were all closely examined to plan the most convenient and interesting route. A general plan began to evolve whereby five of us went off together to the island of Komodo stopping on the way there and back at any interesting locations. After that, when Mark and Harry returned to their business in London, I would use the boat again to make a more detailed search in the eastern section of the Nusa Tengara islands for a suitable place for the refugees. In-between the two sailing trips I wanted to visit west Timor and the interior of Flores - one of the larger islands in the group.

After our nautical tuition Mark and Harry had gone straight on to Bali to supervise the conversion of the boat they had bought. It was twenty feet long and built from the single log of a forest giant from Kalimantan. It was designed and used for transporting cows between Bali and Lombok, and hence had a deep draught in comparison with a fishing boat. On either side of the boat were two outriggers supporting a bamboo float as long as the boat itself and essential for stability.

Meanwhile I was dealing with a checklist of marine items recommended by Denise St Aubyn Hubbard. Charts and other lightweight articles I bought from *Captain O.M. Watts*, a ship's chandler's in London, and decided to look for the more bulky goods in Singapore; this was eventually reduced to foghorn and refills, distress flares, additional charts, pilot book, barometer, sextant and binoculars.

I kept in touch with the activities in Bali, where a sort of double size wooden coffin had been attached to the mid-section of the boat. The boat was only about two feet six inches wide so it extended a couple of feet over each side. Folding doors at either end of the box were intended to keep it cool, but when the front doors were opened sea water sloshed into it so they had to be kept shut, which also meant that the helmsman couldn't see in front of the boat. A thick wedge of foam sponge acted as a mattress, leaving about eighteen inches of headroom; it gave the impression of being in a submarine.

The boat was called the *Baruna Sari*, and to celebrate its conversion, Mark, as the new owner rechristened it the *Gin Pahit*, and appointed himself 'The Commodore' in order to maintain seniority over Made Monoh, the former owner and soon to be our captain. In the event bureaucratic procedures were satisfied with the rank of captain, and Mark's status never officially got beyond Gilbert and Sullivan. Made Monoh and his nephew, John, who was coming as crew, got confused between Mark's title and our destination island of Komodo, and struggled manfully to get their tongues round the distinction until Harry produced a carton of cigarettes also called 'Commodore' - a local brand that smelled like smouldering flipflops - whereupon they gave up and used the same pronunciation to refer to all of them. Eventually of course the 'Komodo', had a 'Komodo' in 'Komodo'.

I arrived in Singapore and was faced with a wide choice of shops, because since it was founded by Stamford Raffles in 1819, it has been a busy and growing port. I went to an area of old shops that I got more pleasure going to than one of the modern emporiums. In fact all of the old parts of Singapore are under threat of becoming a building site and being swept away in a drive to industrialise. Like many people I have mixed feelings about their modernisation programme - the character and flavour that has been lost is offset by being able to arrange things like booking tickets, buying things, and making telephone calls. The Singapore government themselves realised they had overdone it when they bulldozed Bugis Street, and killed off a thriving tourist attraction. As a result they have built a plastic replica in an enclosed concrete arcade, and seem mystified why people don't want to visit it. Of the old hotels, probably the only old one that will survive will be the *Mitre*, and that will be because a high-rise building on the site would overlook Lee Kuan Yew's house and garden.

I selected a shop next to one that had a large faded sign outside saying *Mats, Mosquito Nets, Canvas*; it was clearly from the era of solar topis and gin pahits, and in it I found the atmosphere I liked, with a Chinaman who ended his sentences with the query "You henjoy?", plus a few odds and ends for any jungle travel. In the chandler's next door I bought the goods that we needed for the sailing trip.

Heavily loaded, I flew down to Bali where Mark and Harry in anticipation and enthusiasm had hired a large orange VW jeep, complete with grinning Asian driver, to meet me at the airport and convey the goods down to Sanur and show Captain Made Monoh that we were taking this trip seriously. On the way down they poked through the packets, trying to discover what I'd forgotten.

At Sanur we received an effusive welcome from Made Monoh who lead us down the beach to where the *Gin Pahit* lay chocked under an awning, protecting the workers who were converting it from the hot sun. Next to it was his beach shack, inside of which Mrs Made Monoh and John were sleeping soundly. John with both mouth and eyes open looked strange, and but for the grunts and farts could have been a dead body.

The *Baruna Sari* shortly before being renamed the *Gin Pahit*

Progress was being made with the boat and supplies, leaving the engine as the only other major factor to be solved. We got a lead on this from the owner of a hotel in Sanur called Wia whose family was in the city of Surabaya, and he had kindly contacted them and asked them to have a look round for a suitable forty-horsepower outboard engine. This they had successfully done, so I set off to see if it was okay and buy it if it was. On the way I stopped to visit another Indonesian who owned a pet orang-utan that had been trained to remove girls' clothes at a signal from its owner. Anybody, like myself, who has had physical contact with an orang-utan will know how strong and irresistible they are if they decide to do something. I was mugged by an orang-utan in Sepilok nature reserve in Sabah, and I've seen other people equally manhandled by them.

I duly arrived at a coffee grinding factory in Surabaya where the Chinese in charge had the aforementioned engine strapped to the rim of a forty gallon drum of water so that he could demonstrate it.

The noise of the coffee-grinders, and their operators - a bevy of laughing young girls pouring in the beans - drowned out the noise of the outboard engine, and made it difficult to assess properly. Instead of asking him to stop the grinders or demonstrate the engine on a boat, both of which would have involved a lot of inconvenience - and I was reluctant to do that - so in the best tradition of a *News of the World* reporter, I made my excuses and left.

I then decided it would be better to pay more for the engine but get it from a dealer where in theory I would have redress in the event of the engine malfunctioning or needing repairs. I was soon under the spell of a Chinese shopkeeper who naturally had just the engine for me but whose reluctance to issue any sort of guarantee for even a short period I found hard to reconcile with his insistence on it being such good value. Nevertheless I took the plunge, and in the inflationary world of Indonesia found myself laboriously counting out more than a million rupiahs. Next it had to be sent to Bali, which thankfully the shop arranged with a minimum of fuss, and it arrived just a couple of days later on one of the regular transporters.

Surabaya is the second city of Indonesia, and heavily industrialised. Hundreds of thousands of poor rural people haunt expanding slums to try and get a taste of city life, and yet a short drive brings pleasant open countryside. Wia's family took me into the hills to visit a clove farm, where the sinks of Surabaya seemed hours, not minutes, away. *Sura* means shark and *buaya* crocodile, and the city is founded on the site of a legendary battle between them. In AD 1293 Kublai Khan's Chinese army defeated the Majapahit kingdom of King Wijaya, and the small swampy fishing town began to expand from that time.

After a few hundred years the Dutch colonised it and ran a strict regime until the Japanese invasion in 1942. Although Holland itself was under occupation during the Second World War, they managed to insist that their former possessions should be regained for them by the Allies; thus in 1945, after Indonesian nationalists had gained control of the city, British troops, of all people, fought a three-day battle to recapture the city and hand it over to their old colonial rivals in the area. It was of little point because not long afterwards, the Dutch formally recognised that they couldn't maintain their authority, and granted independence. The legacy of such a messy and humiliating handover is the impertinent and impudent way that the lower orders of Indonesia treat all white people. Every white visitor of whatever nationality will be familiar with the scornful reference of 'Orang Belanda' - Dutchman - and 'Hey, mister' hustling. It used to contrast dramatically with Malaysia, just a border away, where there were no industrial slums and the country had been willingly handed back in 1957, leaving a legacy where white people were called 'Sir', and poverty in the form of industrial slums non-existent. Latterly, to my surprise and disappointment, the increased contact between the two countries' populations, and Malaysia's programme of industrialisation has meant Malaysians being influenced by Indonesians, and picking up some of these bad habits.

During the political upheavals of 1965-66, thousands of communists were massacred by moslem fundamentalists, as indeed happened throughout Indonesia, and there is a widespread feeling that some old scores are waiting to be settled should the opportunity arise. It is similar to the intensity and viciousness of some of the revenge killings in Yugoslavia. For example during the Second World War, Catholic Croatians and Bosnian Moslems sided with the Nazis, denounced Orthodox Serbs who supported the Allies, and were responsible for thousands of Serbs being put in camps and killed. Now the boot is on the other foot and the Serbs are taking their understandable, if not acceptable, revenge.

I got back to Bali in time to receive the wooden crate containing the engine. Mark, Harry and myself then transported it to Sanur to seek Made's comments. We hauled the wooden crate into position and with considerable anticipation all of us pulled the crate apart. There it lay, a gleaming 40HP Tomatsu. It was intended to be used in emergencies and for manoeuvring in awkward coral studded areas. We turned to Made Monoh for an intelligent comment and, as far as I was concerned, confirmation that I had made a good buy.

However he pulled a face of resigned disappointment and started mentioning all sorts of uncomplimentary things about it that seemed irrelevant. I assumed he felt obliged to say something carping in order to justify his new and exalted role as captain of three whitemen, and busied myself trying to find the promised spare parts and toolkit amongst the packing debris. Mark and Harry meanwhile looked grim as the catalogue of faults that Made was listing became longer and more complicated. He pointed, patted, gesticulated and occasionally laughed good-naturedly to show that he was only trying to be helpful.

I soon discovered that, first, none of the tools or spares had arrived and so I could legitimately become a target on that account, and secondly that Made had never actually owned or even used an outboard engine but had merely picked up gossip from a Frenchman on whose boat he had acted as crew and in the Sanur Warungs where the local fisherman gathered to socialise; so it was agreed that Tommy Tohatsu should be given a chance to prove itself.

However Made's wobbly knowledge of engines was more than compensated for by his seamanship, diving ability, energy, general good humour, and willingness to convert his old boat to something along our specifications. It had been high up on the foreshore in his village near Sanur for several weeks and he had been carrying out the conversion work with enthusiasm. His simple family house was made of wood and atap, with shade trees and some domestic animals foraging around it. Underneath the doorstep lived one of the mangy ubiquitous Balinese dogs that showed its teeth in a trembling sneer if one approached beyond its invisible boundary.

Work was progressing well: the small cabin overhanging the gunnels was complete and it provided a dry area for four people to sleep at one time, and the equipment was stored below. Inside it the smell of freshpaint guaranteed that it would soon be renamed the 'vomitorium'. A thick layer of sponge foam had been put on the floor which reduced the headroom to a few inches. Two opening doors at the far end were the only way the helmsman could see straight in front of the boat and this visibility was further reduced if somebody was lying inside; and as a final conundrum at times when visibility was most needed the weather necessitated the closing of the doors.

Petrol for the engine was stored in plastic jerrycans underneath the foam floor in an awkward configuration that caused John Roben's cigarettes to shower sparks over them whenever he wrestled with one of the heavy cans. The rudder, the mast, and the sail were all rigged according to local practice and quite unlike anything in the West; nearly everything we had learnt from Captain Denise was clearly inappropriate and our 'competent crew' certificates issued for Chichester harbour were to be of limited use.

The two large bamboo outriggers were secured to four swan-necked wooden davits which Mark eyed thoughtfully and rechristened "outshitters". His perspicacity was debateable as in the event they provided only a marginally more suitable perch than anything else on the boat. Crouched like a jockey on the bucking bamboo float, hands grasping the wooden davit it needed the concentration of Boris Spassky to perform.

This had raised the question of laxatives and when Mark's huge waterproof fish box of medical supplies - prepared by an experienced expeditionary doctor - had proved not to contain any, as well as many other commonplace medicaments, we began to question exactly what was inside it. A beautifully typed list was produced from a plastic waterproof cover and he read out a list of everything from antiserum for a black-widow spider bite to complicated equipment for performing minor operations. The fish-box at once became a standing joke and I felt a tinge of regret when I heard it had sunk without trace when another boat Mark was on had been broken up on the remains of a half-submerged Japanese wreck in Honiara harbour.

As well as providing the fish-box of medical supplies Mark had taken a short medical course, and in order to reassure us he demonstrated how he would deal with a gashed leg. An orange took the place of the leg and Mark quickly produced scissors, needle and thread, but from then on, when two needles had been snapped, another bent almost in half, the orange lacerated to the specifications of a Chelsea football supporter knifing a rival fan after a home defeat, and the knots in the stitches scarcely doing justice to somebody wearing boxing gloves, it became clear his medical course was on a par with his nautical one.

In a class of its own

# *Chapter 2*

## *Setting Off*

The morning we left, one of the many Balinese who had been taking a passing interest in our activities sent his sister and cousin up to the house bearing extra floral offerings for the deities to ensure us a smooth departure. Even at the launch site joss sticks had been stuck in the sand. A large number of fishermen were on hand to lift the boat into the water and a final offering was pressed onto us to throw into the channel leading through the reef. A small crowd of locals and tourists had gathered to watch the departure attracted by the large amount of baggage that we had assembled over the last few days as we kept on thinking of new 'indispensable' items.

Tommy roared into life and with a graunching noise Made slammed it into gear before the revs had died down, causing Mark, who was standing legs astride waving to his tearful Chilean girlfriend, to topple into the water; he just had time to grab the edge of an outshitter and was unceremoniously dragged through the break in the reef as we threw out the offerings. Once in calmer water we reorganised ourselves and discovered after a "haven't you got it?" exchange that the boat's papers and custom forms had been left behind. Back we went through the reef, passing the remains of the offering that was bobbing up and down next to Mark's hat to a lot of ribald laughter from the people on the beach.

By 3.30 in the afternoon we had assembled the various documents plus the compass and barometer which we discovered had also been forgotten and made a second, more low-key, departure. Mostly using the motor we crossed over to Lembongan island in about four hours. Made had some family here who fed us arak and fried rice which, combined with the strain of getting off and the unfamiliarity of being aboard, sent us off for an early night.

Lembongan seemed a beautiful island and less populated than Bali, perhaps only a few hundred acres against Bali's 144km length, 80km width and three million people. Close by rose the steep forbidding cliff faces of Nusa Penida; in contrast to Bali, it's dry, arid and supports little vegetation. In past days it was used as a place of banishment for undesirables from Bali.

From Lembongan we sailed north-east which brought us back to the coast of Bali and to an area on the island that is all but inaccessible except by boat. We made our way slowly up the coast, taking it in turns to get out of the sun inside the small cabin with its one foot of headroom that was further imperilled by sharp-edged wooden struts. Suddenly Harry let out a cry "Warung ahoy", and John Roben steered the boat towards the shore from where a local canoe soon put off to bring us back to the village. A *warung* is a cross between a pub and a coffee house but we applied it to any establishment, public or private that might supply sustenance. The villagers weren't particularly friendly and it soon became obvious what they expected from us when they pointed out that the fare back to our boat would be an exorbitant sum, so we swam slowly back to the boat holding our money above our heads with one hand.

We decided to make our way across the Lombok trough to the island of Lombok in the evening. This passage also marked the 'Wallace Line' where Asian flora and fauna becomes Australasian flora and fauna. The deep trough between the two islands also poses a further intermittent hazard known as the 'Ripples' when strong currents from the south surge through the strait and meet counter currents confused by the numerous islands in the archipelago. There doesn't seem to be any way of predicting when the ripples are likely to occur so we put ourselves firmly in the hands of Made and squashed into the vomitorium to get some rest. The swim out from the village had left us with a coating of salt and an unpleasant 'hairshirt' sensation so a lively debate developed on whether the jerry-cans of fresh water could be used to wash it off or whether they should be husbanded for cooking and drinking only. We agreed to defer the decision till later.

The morning found us off the coast of Lombok, which was mountainous and predominantly brown, with splashes of green in the valleys and gullies on the hillsides. Made informed us that the winds had been against us which had made for slow progress. Sweeping the shore with our binoculars we could make out a knot of sleepy villagers sprawled under a palm-leaf shelter. We decided to test how easy it was to get water and petrol in order to guage the extent to which we could use it, so we made our way into the bay and anchored within sight of a small fishing village. The shore was very steep and small canoes lined the ridge in front of the village. We gave a few shouts and waved in a friendly way and eventually curiosity got the better of two of the slumbering figures, and by slow degrees a flimsy-looking canoe with one outrigger made its way out to the boat, piloted by a pot-bellied youth wearing a french beret.

Once ashore we discovered that it was the Moslem fasting month of Ramadan so that arranging anything during the day was virtually impossible, but by now most people had woken up and were lazily yawning and scratching themselves as they wondered whether to assist us. Eventually one of them who owned a motorcycle said he was going into the nearest town anyway and would see if he could fill up one jerrycan of petrol. This took so long that we decided to abandon the idea of filling up any more cans. As it was, the flimsy canoe sank just as it arrived back with the can of petrol, so we were stuck with the youth wearing a french beret until another canoe could be persuaded to pick him up and tow the semi-submerged canoe back.

We then decided to sail a little further up the coast and wait until the evening, when we hoped to be able to find some activity in the nearest town. We duly went ashore a few miles up the coast in a pleasant bay with some shade trees and consumed some Bintang beer. Made and John stayed on board to look after the boat and get some rest. Made had great stamina and seemed to be able to go all day and night without a break and insisted that he was happy doing so. John Roben was more human managing only a few hours at a stretch while we were thoroughly unpracticed which, combined with the sea air and hot sun, made us as drowsy as a fasting Moslem. Made preferred to sail at night when the winds were better and it wasn't so hot, but naturally we wanted to sail during the day to see as much as possible.

On the horizon behind the *Gin Pahit* were several local sailing craft laboriously tacking backwards and forwards but scarcely making any headway. Indonesia is one of the last places where widespread commercial sailing is still carried on and the famous wooden *macassar* schooners crisscross the archipelago for months and even years at a time before returning to their home ports. Suddenly our reveries were disturbed by the appearance of a deer-hunting party with rusty spears and three mangy dogs with bells round their necks for some inexplicable reason. After the usual pleasantries we questioned the leader about the distance to the nearest town and made the mistake of phrasing it in such a way that he was able to give the answer that he thought we wanted to hear. "Is it ONE kilometre?" we had asked keenly.

"Yes, yes," he had answered, and with relief we had bid him happy hunting and made our plans accordingly as the tinkling of the bells on the dogs' collars disappeared into the distance.

Loaded with a couple of jerrycans apiece we set off in the direction he had indicated. After about two hours' walking and allowing for the fact that an Indonesian kilometre might be longer than that in other places, it was obvious that for whatever reason we had been led astray and unless we got on the local wavelength soon we were going to have a frustrating time. After about three hours and in no mood to be messed around any further we trundled into the sleepy town and in response to our questions on where to get water and fuel Mark and Harry were told to stop smoking because it was contrary to 'fasting' regulations.

We now had the first of many earnest discussions on what would be the most effective way of achieving our goal of acquiring fuel and water - the direct approach, the indirect one, grovel, be friendly, or polite but distant. Much depended on who we were talking to and how we were feeling at the time, and it was important to get it right first time because the line between success and failure was a narrow one. Having finally got the jerrycans filled up we realised that we couldn't return to the boat the way we had come, and instead hired a *bemo* - a sort of pick-up truck priced midway between a taxi and a bus - to take us to the nearest point on the coast and then, following a lengthy bargaining session with the local headman, got ferried along the coast to the *Gin Pahit* where Made and John were fully recuperated and looking forward to setting off at about 9 o'clock that evening; it was already about 7.30 p.m. Exhausted by our efforts we were ready to agree to anything so we crawled into the vomitiorium, each of us clipping the top of his head on the protruding wooden strut and letting out an oath, and went snoring off to sleep.

At 4 o'clock the following morning a commotion in the cockpit turned out to be Mark announcing that he was going to "slam us across the Alas Strait". This strait divided Lombok from Sumbawa, and Mark in the driving seat had a touch of Toad of Toad Hall about him. Made naturally deferred to 'The Commodore', but clearly expended more energy nannying us than doing things himself. The sail was duly rolled up, the engine started and off we went in the direction of Sumbawa island. The rigging on the boat meant that the sail had to be rolled up instead of pulled down so that in a strong wind it was a minimum two-man job - one to hold the boat into the wind keeping any pressure off the sail as the other person rolled it up.

We made easy progress motoring although the noise of the engine was unpleasant, and when a gentle breeze began which made it convenient to sail in a north-easterly direction towards Moyo island we stopped the engine and altered course to it. The current however had different ideas and presently we found ourselves heading for Maddang island, which we decided would be the new destination.

As we had only been going for a short time, we hadn't yet sorted out where to put things, and a plastic dustbin that we had lashed to the top of the cabin as a temporary measure to store things had already assumed a semi-permanent role. Inside were goggles, spear-guns, ketchup, cutlery, biscuits, peanuts, cigarettes, joss-stick offerings, binoculars and everything else that was used regularly. The washing fluttered from wherever it could be tied, like bits of rubbish on a wire fence behind a jetstream. It wasn't a shipshape boat. Next to the dustbin was our own *warung* consisting of a paraffin stove shaded on three sides with plywood. John Roben was in charge of it and, apart from a knack of getting kerosene into the coffee had a repertoire of one - rice and fish. If we were lucky it was fresh fish, if not, tinned fish.

Kampong Merit, Flores Island.

As we approached Maddang island the wind and tide began to shift again; it looked as though we wouldn't make it, so on went Tommy and we powered towards it. The easy earlier pace had made us casual about securing various loose articles and in a moment the *warung* top, two pillows and a bucket, various knives and forks, several shirts and hats flew overboard. "Keep going" somebody shouted, but Made wheeled round and recovered the top of his beloved *warung* and a saturated pillow. Everything in the vicinity of the *warung* was greasy and filthy, and this prompted a cleaning exercise coupled with an attempt to 'air' the foam sponge and anything else that was 'airable'. Made continued to complain about the engine but it kept going.

Maddang island had several villages on it and many of the villagers were fishing among the reefs. We dived there and entered the alluring world of a coral reef. Harry descended to the coral depths armed with a powerful spear gun and huge knife strapped to his ankle, ready to battle any sort of sea monster, but he had been unprepared for a piece of stationary coral, and scraped some skin off his back. The immediate soreness was compounded by his anticipation of the wound turning septic.

From here our destination was Bima, the main town on the island of Sumbawa; we motored past Moyo island which was forested and Satonda island which according to the pilot book had a salt water lake in a crater in the middle of the island. These sort of details supplied by the pilot book, I put in the back of my mind for future reference, although they rarely proved to be of any use.

Made's superhuman efforts at the helm, combined with John's cooking, had effectively sealed him up and it was at this stage that we discovered the famous fish-box didn't contain laxatives. Terra firma and privacy were prescribed and Tommy took us screaming towards Kananga village on a narrow strip of wooded land at the foot of Tamborah volcano on Sumbawa island. We arrived just after dusk so that the inhabitants had broken their fast and were up and about. We asked about petrol and water and they said an Australian timber-contractor was just round the coast and could supply us with what we needed; the only thing was, they explained, they needed to show us exactly how to reach it. We were all for going but Made saved us from blundering into another wasted effort by saying they probably wanted to get a lift round there and we were almost certain to find that there *had* been a timber contractor there a few years ago or some other excuse for there being no petrol and water. Detracting from this argument was the fact that Made's bowels had taken charge, and they weren't going any further until they had produced some results. This apparently took until about 2.30 a.m. when we heard John being shaken awake by Made and shortly afterwards we slipped anchor. We sailed and motored according to the wind and currents and at dawn entered Dompo bay, at about the same time the fishing line that was being trawled snapped taut and by degrees a five-foot tuna was landed to provide the fresh fish variety of our diet for the next day or two. Such was the size of the fish that an innovation was added to our diet whereby sections of it were dried in the sun to provide palatable preserved rations, but the smell was not a success.

On shore Tamboroh volcano was surrounded by fractured hillsides where wild ponies grazed. These ponies appeared all over the island and the islanders used them for domestic purposes; no doubt everybody knew to whom each pony belonged but there were no fences. The volcano had erupted in 1815 and again in 1895 when 20,000 people were killed.

There was some heavy chop in Dompo bay, apparently completely localised, and no doubt another example of currents clashing as they swirled around the hundreds of islands and coral heads. We headed on towards Bima and by 6 o'clock Made wanted to anchor for the night, but the thought of a cold beer and a hotel room, however grotty, was too much for us, and we pressed on up the narrow channel that leads to Bima with the feeble light from our torches sweeping the water in front of us in an attempt to illuminate any potential danger. Philippe the Frenchman for whom Maday had worked had written us a note urging us never to overrule Made's advice - but what could we do in circumstances like these?

However, we arrived without mishap and after three attempts to anchor got in the right position so that we could wade ashore, but by then it was too late in the evening and everything had closed up for the night.

# *Chapter 3*

## *Komodo Dragons*

Bima is a solidly Moslem town and the inhabitants fought for an independent Moslem state at the time of independence from the Dutch, and the setting up of the Indonesian state, culminating in 1957 in an assassination attempt on President Sukarno which resulted in thirteen schoolgirls being blown up. The guide book referred to the possibility of getting stoned (with rocks) for such things as 'dressing incorrectly', and the local hotels as being 'extremely nasty'. It clearly wasn't a port designed for sailors to spend their rest and relaxation in, but it was a welcome change from the confines of the boat. We were up with the first shafts of dawn light ready to face the inevitable police checkpoint at the harbour entrance. They took possession of the boat's papers for inspection and then equally inevitably darkly suggested that money was required to get them back. Leaving that problem to fester for a time we wandered into the dusty street to be immediately accosted by a youth wielding a phrasebook saying "Let's go together".

"Let's not" was our unanimous reply, but clearly he didn't understand and kept repeating the phrase and following us around until we shooed him away. I was reminded of a passage I had just read in a book: 'An Arab carpet seller - the same one I think who sold us the prayer rug at the Negresco - tried to liven us up, but Henry dealt with him in his best Empire-destroying manner, telling "the dam' nigger to buzz off".'

Everywhere there were small carts called *dokars* pulled by emaciated ponies that presumably had been grazing quietly, contentedly and well fed on the island's hillsides before being pressed into service as workhorses. The drivers of these carts, with smooth, sallow complexions and surly expressions, struck the rumps of these unfortunate animals with a bamboo stick in exactly the same spot, thereby creating a raw patch and facilitating their task of inflicting maximum discomfort for minimum effort from themselves. There were very few cars and it came as no surprise to find that there wasn't a single petrol station in this the largest town on the island. Instead Pertamina, the state oil company, had a depot a few miles out of town and it was from here that people had to get their petrol, if they had stocks, which needless to say, on the day we arrived, they hadn't.

We turned our attention to the water and engaging a *dokar* we took our jerrycans down to the town well and waited our turn to fill them up. Going back to the boat we made our best efforts at making friends with the harbour police, taking their photographs, promising to send them copies, telling them that Bima was good, the harbour was good, they were good, Indonesia was good, and although we raised smiles and handshakes out of them, our documents remained in their office with an unspecified tariff required to release them.

The atmosphere of the town was straight from the Middle East with the dry dusty streets, men in cotton nightdresses and embroidered waistcoats with white or black songkoks and the odd tarboosh on their heads, while the few women abroad were shrouded in black drapes. The houses were simple adobe boxes with windows facing into courtyards rather than onto the street. There was a central market with pungent vegetables laid out or heaped in rattan baskets, many kinds of snackettes and dried things smelling predominantly of dried prawns; the market was shaded on four sides with an open centre above which an attempt had been made to provide shade by suspending pieces of sewn-together gunny sack like washing hanging out to dry. At one end men in checked sarongs and for some reason peaked caps, sold hardware with other sundry items such as plastic buckets; hand baggage, shoes, combs, mirrors, and umbrellas were hanging overhead. At the other end mainly women had a wide variety of fruit and vegetables laid out.

The delay over the petrol prompted us to stay at the Komodo Inn which was a long low building with a terracotta tiled roof and a row of simple but surprisingly cool rooms. In the 'foreign quarter' of the town there were many other buildings similar in design which echoed either the missionary or Dutch influence. Most were two-storey with louvred windows and exterior shutters; trees stood around them or in the compounds, or more usually there were the remains of where they had been standing until they were cut down after independence.

The Komodo Inn provided the first chance to have a proper wash. However, Harry had taken a brave decision - having finally settled down with a coating of salt he didn't want to start all over again and elected not to wash in fresh water until he got back to Bali. While scooping water over myself from the concrete trough in the bathroom, an inquisitive rat emerged to see what was going on. A well aimed shot with the soap sent it back into the drain.

The following day it became clear that we weren't the only people waiting to get petrol. Many others were waiting outside the Pertamina depot and when by some invisible signal a few hours later the petrol became available there was a mad scrimmage to try and get to the front of the crowd before this particular ration ran out; by dint of there being three of us we managed to bulldoze our way to the front and fill up four jerrycans but not all of what we wanted. This incident also highlighted the problem of acquiring fuel in this group of islands - if we had this problem in the main town of one of the biggest islands we were obviously going to have to fill up a can here and there whenever we could.

Mark and me making friends in the hope they'll forget about the paperwork

When that failed Mark borrowed one of their toys to emphasise the point

Back at the harbour a macassar schooner loaded with potatoes and ponies was slowly drifting out on the tide bound for Balikpapan, Made and John were making any little repairs that needed doing, and close by a Western yacht had appeared; on it was a middle-aged Australian called Ian Whitton who had just been having a refit in some Asian port and was on his way back home to Evans Landing in Queensland. His original crew had been two Australians but as is the way with boat crews they changed, and in his case they had got off in Bencoolen in Sumatra and been replaced by a local policeman who apparently had suggested a 'joyride' instead of baksheesh for some bureaucratic infringement and then stayed on; Ian had worked on pearling luggers around Broome in Western Australia before the War and after it had spent fourteen years as a plantation manager in the Solomon islands and then varying periods in other islands of the south-west Pacific. Taking everything into consideration he found Indonesia the most pleasant place to sail in, and suggested that Wetar island to the north of East Timor might be a suitable place for the Vietnamese refugees. As there was a war going on in East Timor at the time, between Indonesia and the former inhabitants of Portuguese Timor, it sounded a bit hazardous, and as far as the Vietnamese were concerned merely swapping one war zone for another, but once again I filed it away in the back of my mind.

Made, who had been against the idea of sailing up the Bima channel at night, now felt confident enough to sail out at night and proposed an evening departure; Ian thought this sounded very strange but rightly or wrongly we put our faith in 'local' expertise, and after paying the harbour police armfuls of money to retrieve the boat's papers, got ready to leave. For the actual departure somebody lit a hurricane lamp with the idea of seeing where we were going. Naturally enough this merely had the opposite effect; we could see nothing while everybody else could see what we were doing. Almost at once from the darkness outside our halo of light an excited chatter swiftly increased in volume until there was a bump, a creak of straining wood, and the person with the hurricane lamp fell flat on their face and the lamp splashed hissing into the water and immediately extinguished. Once our eyes had become accustomed to the darkness we established that minor damage had been done to one of the outriggers while the macassar schooner into which we had run had suffered no damage at which point their crew started laughing noisily. Made and John swiftly carried out the necessary repairs, and away we went.

In the morning we were surrounded by a lot of small islands and rock outcrops; the currents were very strong and clearly the one thing to avoid was the engine cutting out and our boat being repeatedly slammed into the rocks. Almost on cue Tommy coughed a few times and died in a last gasp of spluttering noise. Now we were all involved. Harry who had tied himself to the roof untied himself and looked as thoughtful as one could under the circumstances, I wrestled with a life jacket and prepared to be the first rat to leave the sinking ship, Mark meanwhile became the hero of the piece: removing the engine cover, he tinkered with a few rubber hoses, declared that he had reattached the fuel line to the carburettor and asked Made to "start her up again". He was like the Walter Mitty hero who replaced a tube in a faltering machine in an operating theatre with the inner tube of his fountain pen. A couple of tugs of the starting cord, and with the boat bobbing vulnerably on the steeply undulating waves only a few metres from the rocks, the engine burst into life and we made our way round the point. Contrary to Made's earlier predictions, Tommy had been behaving so well that even he had been lulled into a false sense of security and been caught out. As this was already Komodo island I imagine that if we had been cast upon the barren rocks a hungry dragon would have been waiting for us. The pilot book was not content with just dragons, it referred to thirty-foot sea-water crocodiles patrolling the shorelines.

Having rounded the southern tip of Komodo island the sea was calmer and an accommodating breeze started so that we could sail for a bit. John Roben was tired out by being up all night and coughed and shivered until we allowed him into the vomitorium for some rest. Made was as bright as ever and rounded off a sterling performance by catching a large tuna. As we made our way along Komodo the barren, rocky, fissured landscape was unbroken. Dense scrub covered the hillsides, and green was only evident in the gullies where the rain water was channelled. In contrast the beaches with white sand and clear water looked inviting until one remembered the thirty foot crocodiles.

We landed at the only village on Komodo, a former penal colony, in the late afternoon and announced our desire to find the dragons. Various fasting villagers nodded disinterestedly and we retired to an island opposite the village to cook up the fish and prepare for the next day's expedition. We read and reread the pilot book, the Indonesian handbook and various other articles that we had brought, concerning the best way to approach the business of dragon-hunting and decided that some rotting meat placed in a strategic location was the way to go, but we retired to bed without deciding on the important questions of where to get the rotten meat, how to get it to its location and who would place it in the tempting position, although a general consensus reached was that John Roben might have been able to serve all three functions.

Early the next morning before the villagers had a chance to slip into the day's torpor we landed at the village and were gratified to find that far from facing the problem of making ourselves understood the people were well used to dealing with people such as ourselves and had already organised a goat and a couple of people to bring it. They explained that we would have to travel round the coast a little way in our boat and then walk for a while, "Oh, and um that will be 25,000 rupiahs altogether, thank you."

We all squashed onto the Gin Pahit and motored round to the starting-off point, and then strode off into the scrub following our two guides. About twenty minutes later we were shown a place to lie and wait, in front of a natural viewing area at the bottom of a sharp incline. The incline provided some reassurance against the dragons suddenly turning their attention from the goat to us but what if the dragons approached the bait from behind us? We weren't left to ponder this possibility for long because no sooner had the villagers positioned the goat than a twelve foot dragon appeared from the undergrowth and began devouring the goat; shortly afterwards a wild boar also appeared and managed to drive the dragon off for a few moments before another large dragon appeared followed by two more smaller ones. The boar was outnumbered and disappeared back into the scrub and then a couple of smaller dragons did indeed appear behind us and we decided to move our positions before a larger one came. The guide book referred to the dragons' pungently bad breath resulting from their diet of rotting food, so in the interests of science we sent Made forward to check on this.

"You'll be quite safe," we told him, "they're far too busy with the goat."

But they weren't and curiosity got the better of one of them; at first Made made a feeble attempt to shoo it away but that seemed to interest it further and he sprang into the branches of a nearby tree.

"Not there," we shouted, "the guide book says they can climb trees," and at that the dragon lumbered up to the tree, goat's entrails still hanging from the corners of its mouth, and looked ready to have a go, but to Made's relief it decided that with a full stomach already it was just too much effort. It soon sauntered off and Made was able to rejoin us and confirm that its breath was indeed very unpleasant.

Our blameless goat goes the way of all flesh

Presently we returned to the boat where John Roben had been keeping a lookout and sailed back to the village, and then to our island offshore.

Looking at Komodo island from the point of view of resettling people, it seemed that there was certainly plenty of space, and the climate was pleasant; but on the negative side there wasn't much water and the soil appeared poor and dusty, although it was in an area of volcanic activity and perhaps if the water problem could be overcome by energetic Vietnamese the land could blossom. The surrounding islands all supported substantial populations and that in spite of inefficient land management. Komodo had traditionally been left alone because of the dragons and its reputation as a penal colony so maybe its hour had come. I wanted to look at the far side of the island to see if it had the same sort of topography, but was saved from actually having to go round there by the unexpected visit of two Europeans. A small boat came over to our island with an Englishman called Lorne Blair and a French colleague, plus somebody who said he was half Balinese, half English - whether literally or figuratively I didn't discover. They had been filming the dragons on the far side of the island as part of a six part series for the BBC on Indonesia called *Ring of Fire*, they had heard via the bush telegraph that we were around and wanted to see what we were doing. They were able to cap most of our stories, including that of the dragons, by relating how they were so intent on filming them that they had approached practically to the end of the camera lens because of the naturally elongated view that the lens gave. At the last minute they had had to scurry into the bush, they also considered that our dragons were well fed 'tourist' ones and weren't much danger, Made wasn't able to understand this otherwise I'm sure he would have had something to say. On the question of topography, yes, it was much the same on the other side of the island. I didn't then mention Vietnamese refugees as I'm sure the Frenchman would have already been involved in some esoteric resettlement programme in a far flung corner of the globe and would have proceeded to point out all the difficulties. Instead they became interested in the route we had taken and it soon became the turn of the Bugis captain of their chartered macassar schooner to tell us how crazy we had been. Made was able to understand this but appeared to be too busy carrying out a minor repair to join in the discussion.

Before Lorne left I discovered that his filming in Borneo had included visiting a remote Penan village with a ginger-haired girl, which I had also visited, and I was interested to subsequently see her and the village on the film 'in the comfort of my own armchair'. The same applied to the episode on Komodo which brought back this occasion.

# Chapter 4

## *Paternoster Islands*

From Komodo we decided to sail to Reo on the island of Flores and from there to head north to a group of islands in the middle of the Flores Sea of which the largest was Tana Jampea. The pilot book described it as being high and thickly wooded and indented on the west side, off which lay several small islands. It also referred to only two small villages as most of the islanders preferred to seek work on either the larger islands sixty miles to the south or in the Celebes, a similar distance to the north. This was the sort of location I was looking for.

Using the engine it took just a morning to travel from Komodo to Labuanbajo on the west coast of Flores, passing Padar island, Rinja island and many other smaller ones, all of which looked ideal for settlement purposes. Labuanbajo was an interesting mixture of Islam and Roman Catholicism. Simple churches and mosques stood almost side by side and little girls dressed as brownies contrasted with the drapes of the moslem faithful. Even the boats seemed to suggest a divided community with strangely constructed catamarans beside the normal Buginese fishing vessels. After a trouble-free session completing formalities with the local police officer we were directed to the 'Komodo office' which was run by a friendly Roman Catholic. After filling us up with strong coffee he arranged for us to get petrol from the local chinese towkay. Suddenly we were back in the system with the right bits of paper and everything was easier; we knew it wouldn't be long before we were out of the system again through not following some procedure, and the hassles would start again. We said *à bientôt* to the heavy-metal kid in the police station and set off up the coast for about two miles, anchored there, and spent the rest of the day trying to spear some fish or other edible crustaceans. John was under the weather again and spent the day and following night lying in the vomitorium. His disturbing feature of sleeping with his eyes half open as though he was continually watching and assessing, had continued, and was not the one-off anomaly that we had thought when we first found him asleep in Sanur.

Flores appeared to be less barren than the other islands. Coconut trees lined the white beaches, and behind them as far as and including the low-lying hills, the predominant impression was one of green. At midday we called into Merit village which again had Malay type inhabitants divided between Roman Catholocism and Islam. On some fishing boats on the foreshore were groups of negroid types who presumably had come from further east although it was relatively unusual to find these sort of people working as itinerant traders. The atmosphere in this village was friendlier than most, perhaps because they had a marginally more varied diet, and we managed to buy some bananas, bread and sardines.

We soon pushed on towards Reo where a cruising shark greeted us just inside the bay. We then got in a slight muddle trying to work out where the town was, at first confusing it with the port of Kedindi. Once again the prospect of spending the evening ashore urged us to press on despite darkness falling, so by the time we located the river-mouth visibility was very limited. We spotted another boat on the far side of the river and deciding that that was the way to go went hammering over there only to find ourselves suddenly decelerating very rapidly to a full stop. We had run aground on a mud bank and the other boat was already well aground itself. We all crawled into the vomitorium to get some sleep until the incoming tide floated us off. Later in the evening we gingerly made our way upriver to the town. There was no landing place, just a muddy river bank but we scrambled up it and descended on the local *warung* where the only alcoholic beverage on sale was a local Chinese brandy called John Roben. This was where John had acquired his nomenclature, and to celebrate his baptism we sang 'Tom Dooley' substituting the name 'John Roben'. Made and John pronounced it John-Robin, and the name stuck. Despite visiting scores of *warungs* this was the first appearance of John Roben whisky. However latterly the brand has been re-promoted with new labels and sits proudly on supermarket shelves. Who was John Roben? Perhaps a Dutch beachcomber living in Reo before the War who brewed it up as a hobby, or a relative of the Lancashire bard Tim Boben, after whom a pub is named in south London.

There had obviously been a strong Dutch presence here originally. A large corrugated-iron cathedral dominated the town and Dutch nuns had returned here and were teaching in the schools and generally assisting in local life. Reo was little more than a village, there were no roads from here to anywhere else and all around were forest-covered hills; it had a nice atmosphere and its port of Kedindi was just a beach at the end of a bay with a jetty extending into the sea. The Protestants were also represented here but nobody we spoke to seemed to be putting down their rivals, so on appearances at least there was mutual harmony. The Moslem fasting month had just ended and we were invited to a local celebration to sip warm, sweet drinks and nibble garishly coloured sweetmeats; not a bottle of John Roben was in sight so on our way back we bought the last case of it, to the delight of the shopkeeper, and stored it lovingly in the bottom of the boat.

Our plan from Reo was more ambitious as it meant sailing sixty miles from the coast and would involve some navigation. In retrospect I'm surprised at our confidence that everything would work out and there was no doubt an element of collective security where we thought Made could deal with any situation, while *he* got carried along by our enthusiasm and was impressed by the charts and gadgets that we had brought along. Trying to set a course in an area where the currents were strong and unpredictable, the winds on the whole light and unpredictable in a craft that had no keel and was therefore liable to exaggerated lateral movement, with none of us having any practical experience of navigation, should have called for caution combined with optimism; but we had a discussion over a glass or two of John Roben as the sun sank behind Reo town and told Made, who had again expressed his intention of setting sail in the middle of the night, to keep the compass pointing at ten degrees, and then retired to bed.

In the morning I woke with a bit of a hangover and incautiously lifting my head banged it into a wooden strut above me. I had recently been sleeping on the roof and got out of the habit of automatically keeping my head low. With a groan I slumped back onto the foam and tried to get back to sleep. A short while later however, Mark crawled out of the fetid coffin, took a brief glance around him, and announced triumphantly that we had arrived; Harry and I struggled out and we all congratulated Made who himself seemed a bit subdued, then however, as we held the charts upside down trying to identify where we were, suddenly discovered that we had merely backtracked down the coast and were off Merit village again. Made obviously hoped that once our indignation had died down and we had given him the benefit of the doubt that the winds were 'susah' (difficult) we might forget about the search for an isolated island and quietly go back to Bali. But we had set our hearts on getting into a whole new area and now studied the chart again to see where we could head for now that we had diverted a significant distance to the west.

Sabalana and Paternoster islands it became. The pilot book mentioned that the 'islands are seldom visited except by chinese junks collecting tripang and by praus from Sulawesi for copra.' Reading further, I noticed it said 'the combined stream is usually strongest along the east and south-east edges of the atolls, in some places attaining a rate of two to three knots for about an hour, with whirlpools and heavy tide rips. It is always advisable for passing vessels to give the edges of the atolls a wide berth".

As we were intending to be a visiting rather than a passing vessel I decided to edit this information when passing it on. I was intrigued to visit the Paternosters as it features in Kipling's poem 'The Mary Gloster'. Made was now replaced at the helm and we steered the new course of 310 degrees. All day we ploughed on towards the horizon and finally towards evening left sight of land; satisfied that we were well on our way we cracked open another bottle of John Roben, and later went to bed anticipating better things the next day.

Once again Mark was first up and noisily announced that we had done it this time. Once again the charts were turned round and around until the truth dawned on us that during the night we had headed almost due west if not south-west and were bobbing off Sangeang island to the north of Sumbawa, in other words another backtrack and that much closer to Bali. Made and John could justifiably claim to be exhausted, that the winds and currents were again 'susah', but it was now going to be a test of wills if, through a few more navigational 'errors', we weren't going to find ourselves back in Bali, and to emphasise this possibility Made said that the winds and currents, and amount of fuel we had left made Bali the obvious choice to head for.

We decided that we had better try and get to the islands before nightfall as none of us volunteered to sleep during the day and be on the helm in the evening. Several jerrycans of fuel were hauled out from the bottom of the boat and we went speeding off in a northerly direction. After a short while we sighted a whale spouting and slowly made our way over to it until one of the outriggers touched its back, but it remained quite disinterested and we were soon on our way again.

Our diet at this point took a turn for the worse in that Made and John-Robin were too tired to fish and as a further ploy to head back to Bali said that the fishing line was wrong for that area, and that the correct tackle had been damaged. Three times a day we had plain boiled rice with a choice of ABC sauce or tomato catsup.

As evening came, there was no sign of any islands and Mark made gallant attempts to climb the stubby mast and get a little extra visibility or spot some lights. By midnight - we had got the bit between our teeth - we calculated that we must have come far enough north and that we needed to make our way slowly to the west. By staying up at night we made the significant discovery that the compass didn't have a light on it and so Made had clearly not been paying any attention to it at all during the previous two nights.

By the early hours of the morning we came to the conclusion that we must have missed the northern group of the islands we were aiming for, and that if we took a south west course we stood a chance of sighting the southern group, and if we missed them then we would carry on in the same direction until reaching the coast of Lombok; so everybody finally went for some rest in the cabin, and I was left to sleepily steer the boat. After about an hour an object resembling the top of a coconut momentarily caught the corner of my eye as it sped past the boat. I happened to turn round to look at it again and was astonished to see the top of Mark's head disappearing into the distance.

"Man overboard!" I bellowed - that much I had remembered from my sailing course. I was then supposed to hurl a buoy into the water to mark the position and give the person something to cling to. We weren't of course equipped with a buoy and no other floatable object was to hand. In that event somebody else was meant to point in the direction of the person in the water and keep pointing while the boat was manoeuvred round, but of course everybody was fast asleep inside the cramped vomitorium. Eventually John, who had been sleeping closest to the cockpit, blearily emerged. I had released the sail as quickly as I could and while it swung about out of control with the sail rope in the water I kept an eye on Mark's position while John started the engine. I was surprised at how quickly the gap between Miark and the boat opened up, until he disappeared in the wave troughs. Then the engine roared into life, we swung round but almost immediately it seized up. The sail rope had become fouled in the propeller. By now however Made and Harry were on the scene and while several pairs of eyes kept a check on Mark's position Made went overboard to untangle the propeller. Presently we were able to pick Mark up and resume our course. It turned out that Mark had crawled through the forward doors, out of sight from the rear of the boat, to relieve himself and so engrossed was he in doing this, combined with fatigue from the night's exertions, had overbalanced into the water. Initially, being submerged, he had had no chance to shout and by the time he was able to, the noise of the wind and the water plus the distance blotted out any sound. Mark was considerably shaken by this narrow escape as he realised that had I been looking the other way or dozing - as I had been through lack of sleep - during the couple of seconds it took for his head to go past the boat, he would certainly have drowned, and as in Kipling's poem, joined Sir Anthony Gloster and his wife at "the heel of the Paternoster".

In another few hours we came up close to a strand of coral reef about fifty yards long by ten feet wide by two feet high. We made a guess, which later proved correct, that it was Karang Satunggul, the eastern extremity of the southern Paternosters. The land area may have been small but the underwater reefs were very extensive and before long we had an impressive collection of crustaceans for the pot which was a great morale-booster.

The following morning we headed for Sapinggang island which had a large area of foul ground growing over the coral on the leeward side. According to the guide book, coral doesn't grow on the leeward side of islands so we were left to ponder that as we struggled across hundreds of yards of drying, dirty weedbanks. On the windward side the reefs were mostly covered in mangrove swamps and on both sides irreversible damage had been done to the reefs from the use of dynamite. There was a community of about a 150 people on the hundred-acre island. There was no possibility of the inhabitants doing anything here other than fishing and producing a little copra. All the buildings were simple leaf roofed huts except for the mosque which had been built with hardwood imported from Banjermasin in Kalimantan.

'Inbred to buggery' is an expression that not only applied to the general look of the people but also had an accepted role in the village. We were ushered along to a hut by an effeminate man who explained when we got there that "only men live here", and then suggested by gesture that we might find attractive a repulsive-looking creature grinning maniacally with zinc covered teeth. However food was upper-most in our minds and we suggested three young coconuts instead, but this change of subject took some time to get across and involved a lot of misunderstood gestures in the early stages that had Zinc-tooth looking alternately alarmed and interested.

Alfred Russel Wallace in his book The Eastern Archipelago (Macmillan & Co. 1869) about the same area describes the people as follows:

"The villages are situated on high and rugged coral peaks, only accessible by steep narrow paths, with ladders and bridges over yawning chasms. They are filthy with rotten husks and oil refuse, and the huts are dark, greasy, and dirty in the extreme. The people are wretched, ugly, dirty savages, clothed in unchanged rags, and living in the most miserable manner; and as every drop of fresh water has to be brought up from the beach, washing is never thought of; yet they are actually wealthy, and have the means of purchasing all the necessaries and luxuries of life. Fouls are abundant, and eggs were given me whenever I visited the villages, but these are never eaten, being looked upon as pets or as merchandise. Almost all of the women wear massive gold earrings, and in every village there are dozens of small bronze cannon lying about on the ground, although they have cost on the average about ten pounds a piece. The chief men of each village came to visit me, clothed in robes of silk and flowered satin, though their houses and their daily fare are no better than those of the other inhabitants. What a contrast between these people and such savages as the best tribes of hill Dyaks in Borneo, or the Indians of the Uaupes in South America, living on the banks of clear streams, clean in their persons and their houses, with abundance of wholesome food, and exhibiting its effect in healthy skins and beauty of form and feature! There is in fact almost as much difference between the various races of savage as of civilized peoples, and we may safely affirm that the better specimens of the former are much superior to the lower examples of the latter class."

Unfortunately the Borneo tribes described above are being forced into the depressed state of the 'lower examples of the latter class' by having their forests logged out.

At the time Wallace was writing the Industrial Revolution was in its infancy. His description of the deleterious effect that factories had on the rural population of England is mirrored in countries that are industrialising now, where the benefits are kept in a few hands. His conclusions tie in with the modern problems dealt with by Brian May in his book the The Indonesian Tragedy. (published in early 1980s).

Wallace pointed out how European goods like scissors were being produced so cheaply in Britain through low wages for export that they were actually cheaper in the most remote places of Indonesia than in Britain itself. A native could sell a shell or feather and buy industrial goods that British workers, working twelve hours a day for a year couldn't afford. The prices should have been much higher and the money distributed back to the British workers but the industrial system with its division of labour, competition and greed made it impossible. Wallace expands on how the richest nations through industrialisation, actually created poverty amongst a large section of the population.

Once a country has adopted an industrial system it is dependent on the supply of raw materials and thereby a hostage to many types of fortune.

Although it is usually stated that industrial countries exploit non-industrial ones by buying raw materials cheaply, my own observations suggest the contrary to be true. Who, for example, has the better deal and stronger hand, the oil consumer or the oil producer?

In May's book, he shows how the Indonesian government's attempt to industrialise with huge grants and cheap loans from the West is creating an identical mass of urban industrial paupers to Victorian Britain, and over the border the same is happening in the Eastern Malay state of Sarawak where previously the Brooke rule had saved the people from this type of exploitation. When the Chief Minister of Sarawak claimed he was creating 50,000 jobs in the logging industry, it wasn't hard to see that really it was 50,000 jobless and homeless he was creating. By cutting down their own forests the natives have a badly paid job for a few months (they spend their wages on beer, and therefore literally piss away their birthright) and then nothing. Furthermore they are killing the goose that lays their golden eggs, because there will be no more forest left to sustain them. They are now faced with joining the newly formed slums around the factories, or disappearing.

May considers that the attempt by the West in partnership with a corrupt local élite to industrialise these countries will have a backlash affect: when the people find that they are worse, not better off, they will blame capitalism and not their own social system. It's hard to escape the conclusion that projects like the Yangste dam in China which cause so much upheaval and destruction serve only to satisfy the megalomania and corruption of bureaucrats and businessmen. Both Wallace and May's concerns are exacerbated by 'cheap loans' and the lack of fear of being defaulters whether as countries or individuals. If people were still boiled in oil for not paying their debts, many fewer loans would be taken out, less 'development' would take place, and the world would generally be a better place as a result.

Our priority was to get some water for which the local 'policeman' tried to extract 5,000 rupiahs per jerrycan, but which came down to 1,000 after some patient negotiating. As expected, it turned out to be fairly brackish even when boiled.

We spent the remainder of the day anchored offshore and Made very skilfully swam and caught a turtle which was another welcome change to our diet. Towards the end of the day a macassar schooner anchored near us and we noticed two canoes putting out from the shore towards it; they delayed briefly and then came paddling over to us. One had people in it asking for cigarettes, the other had Zinc-tooth and two friends in a final attempt to sell themselves; clearly the proclivity of passing sailors was for men, which presumably had developed from Islam's custom of keeping the women penned up.

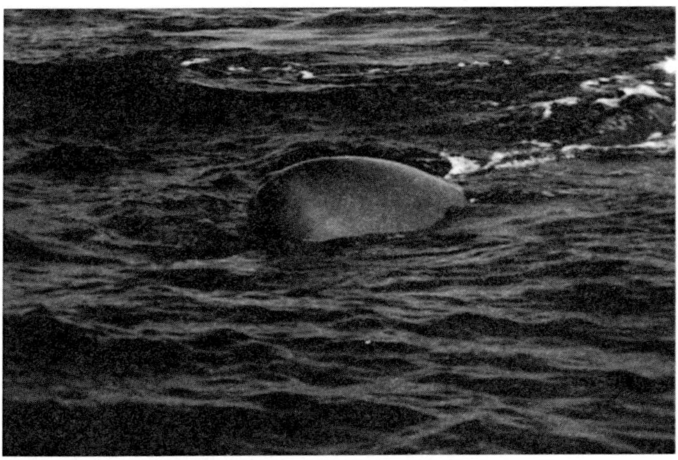

Investigating a friendly whale

We carried on through the chain of reefs, islets and islands. There were some nice-looking beaches surrounding the classic images of a desert island, the sort that is imagined in 'Desert Island Discs'. There aren't of course any seagulls in this part of the world, but the noise of them in the introductory soundtrack to the programme was an attractive anomoly, which unfortunately has been 'corrected'. On every inhabited island a small well built mosque was the most visible sight. Mangrove, dank weedy ground and coral, much of it bombed out, surrounded them. The small canoes mostly had one outrigger, while the larger boats which Made identified as 'turtlers' were made in Kalimantan from hardwoods. Made and John-Robin were generally much happier, as they felt that now we had reached the islands that we were aiming for we would docilely return to Bali.

We stopped at a small empty island with no coconut trees where a pair of eagles was nesting in a fir tree. They didn't seem frightened and gave the impression that had one approached too close or attempted to climb the tree they would have attacked. Even more strangely there were two cats on the island; they miaowed persistently from the shore looking at the boat, indicating that they had had enough of the island and wanted to join us. Our guru, Made, didn't know whether they had been put there for a purpose or just abandoned. There was absolutely no water on the tiny island and food was almost as scarce, so how the cats survived was a mystery. When the Phoenix islands in the central Gilbert islands in the South Pacific were investigated to see whether it was possible to form communities there, rabbits were found apparently living off dew and very poor scrub. Their burrows were so shallow that they could be reached within an arm's length. Another unusual feature of this island were swarms of flies unlike anything we had encountered elsewhere and this was despite a strong wind blowing, so without the wind blowing they would have been unbearable; there were a few coconut trees and a good reef so people must visit the place sometimes. The area had many similar tiny islands with local people clinging to a living.

The next inhabited island, called Makaranangana had houses built on stilts over a drying reef; apparently this facilitated fishing. One of the men living there told me he had never visited the adjoining islands, but as he had a basket of small red onions, bananas, coconuts and some shells sitting in a corner I felt he either misunderstood the question or suspected an ulterior motive and decided to be 'uninvolvable', and in fact when we arrived at the next island we found a certain amount of cultivation such as tapioca and coconuts piled up for 'sprouting', which was clearly his farm. As was usual around this area, there was a lot of foul ground and even some mangrove to wade across before it was possible to go ashore. Once again there were some cats but here it was possible to imagine that there were some tasty rodents around and places where a little fresh water might go.

Although it was getting dark we decided to try and reach the island of Sailus Besar which we had confidently pinpointed on our chart. Apparently coral grows several inches a year so that our charts, which were surveyed up to a hundred years ago and engraved in 1896, could not be considered too reliable although they had been updated at different times. Dusk quickly turned into darkness and the moon not having risen, we were hoping to see pinpricks of light from native oil lamps. The sea began to get choppy although the wind wasn't increasing much and we were clearly in an area of underwater reefs and shallow banks. Suddenly we found ourselves on a breaking sea and the next instant the bottom of the boat was bumping on coral, four of us leapt up while Made shouted instructions which were interpreted differently so that it took us some time and considerable confusion before it seemed safe to anchor. The lack of visibility had been the main hazard. Once again the advantage of having a solid boat with no keel had been demonstrated. Sailing around the archipelago in a keeled boat would either necessitate such caution that the object of any trip would almost be lost or one would have to be very lucky. In both cases it would not do to be worried about such niceties as paintwork or clean decks.

Reo town had produced not only John Roben brandy but also a locally produced cigar which was rolled and packed in wooden boxes for the European market. I don't know what the price would have been once they reached Europe, but here they were about £1 sterling for a box of fifty and they proved to be popular presents although, in the nature of things, a Western cigarette was valued much more highly than the locally produced cigar. It was in our present predicament, anchored on a reef in the middle of the Flores Sea that our thoughts turned unanimously to the above products and we whiled away the next hour or so puffing Sumatran cigars and sipping old John Roben Reo whisky; if it didn't altogether quiet our apprehension we hoped that Made and John were reassured that we had complete faith in their ability to "get us through".

Dawn revealed that Sailus Besar island was not far away and as we eased our way through the foul ground a certain amount of excited activity on the beach indicated that we were either in for a very friendly welcome or were destined for the pot. A sanpan put out from the shore and managed to cover the weedstrewn shallows between where we had been forced to stop and the beach. We wondered whether Zinc-tooth might have got here first and been waiting, grinning horribly, with his sarong hitched dangerously, but there seemed to be no hint of that particular hazard, indeed the whole atmosphere was quite different from the other island only a comparitively short distance away. All the children, girls as well as boys, swarmed around in a friendly way which was reciprocated by the adults.

The island's administration seemed to be under a retiring-looking native struggling under the weight of an ancient rifle, and he remained well in the background despite the derisive taunts of the predominantly youthful crowd to give us the third degree. It was in marked contrast to the usual tinpot official whose life revolves around the opportunity to boss people about and, in the case of Third World countries, white men in particular. The remains of turtles, which Moslems don't usually eat were in evidence and the mosque was not in good repair so I suspect the easier atmosphere had something to do with a correspondingly less rigid religious regime.

Many of the girls' faces were encrusted in a white compound, made apparently from rice, but its purpose seemed obscure to the uninitiated like ourselves. Soon a local dignitary claimed us and we were ushered along to his house built on stilts. More and more people crammed into the first-floor room until it was completely full. Satisfied that he had a proper audience our friendly official ascertained from us that we would like to find out about local currents, places of local interest and the best routes from his island, and would he, er, like to have an influx of Vietnamese refugees on his island or any of the neighbouring under-inhabited ones such as 'Fly island'?

He composed himself in a dignified way, and began talking softly so that everybody had to crane forward to catch the words of wisdom. Then to produce a theatrical effect he became more voluble and, gesticulating expansively, he caused a ripple of movement in his audience which was the fraction of weight redistribution necessary to cause an explosive and complete rending of the wooden supports to half of the floor area. Like a high speed lift most of the room, together with the occupants, whose arms were involuntarily thrust skywards by the sudden release of gravity, disappeared vertically into the damp debris below the house. The remaining audience began laughing which is the usual reaction in Indonesia to any sort of disaster but it didn't indicate genuine mirth. Some people were undoubtedly injured in the fall, as was of course the official's pride, so we groped along a two-inch beam to reach the staircase and prepared for an immediate departure. Moslems can sometimes turn blame in unlikely directions. I remember a Libyan taxi-driver successfully claiming in court damages from his European passenger after he had slammed his taxi into another car, on the basis that if the passenger hadn't requested that route he never would have had the accident.

We had not been able to get any supplies here but it didn't matter, as apart from the house collapsing it had been a pleasant visit. These islands gave the impression that they had space and potential for at least modest resettlement.

We thought we could improve on our hit and miss approach to navigation and our next reference point on the way back to Lombok island was an abandoned lighthouse on Zandbuis Banks. We plotted a course taking account of all the different factors which might affect the boat's direction and set off hoping to arrive in daylight, but the wind or something else didn't do what it was meant to, and we were still ploughing along with our eyes glued to the compass course we had set ourselves when darkness fell. Suddenly we found ourselves surfing over a large reef and landed the other side on some coral; once again we piled out, but this time Made insisted that we get off. We pushed and shoved but jumped back on board with too little depth under the boat and immediately got flung back on the reef again. Most reefs drop away very sharply so that it is difficult to manoeuvre the boat well away from it before jumping aboard. Eventually with Tommy screaming against the noise of the breaking water and some coordinated shoves we got away, but almost immediately slammed into a jagged rock protruding out of the water. Harry was at the front with a torch trying to spot any more hazards and relaying the information to the helmsman, who of course couldn't see forward because of the cabin. By this method we got round to the back of the reef and anchored in some coral. Made and John went diving with waterproof torches, while we unwound with a bottle of vintage John Roben. By the time the alochol had worked up an appetite for us they had resurfaced with some crayfish and other fish, which they cooked up on the paraffin stove in our minute *warung*. During the night some local fishing boats briefly hovered around as though sizing us up but Mark sent them on their way with a stream of pidgin Indonesian. His command of Indonesian for a long time had been one word - makan (food) and he had briefly been referred to as Commodore Makan - but now he had a vocabulary of about twenty words which was enough to satisfy most of what he wanted to say.

In the morning we were greeted with the unexpected sight of some houses on stilts on the eastern section of the banks. Obviously they were used as a base for fishing trips and at high tide they looked strange surrounded on all sides, as far as the eye could see, by uninterrupted water. We sailed on a short distance and found a bank that was just out of the sea and covered in hundreds of nesting terns. On one side of the bank was the wreck of a Maduran boat and looking further along were the remains of the lighthouse. We celebrated our successful piece of navigation by frying our rice ration and supplementing it with crayfish and terns' eggs. This concoction, although tasty at the time, had a bad effect on Harry's stomach and to a lesser extent Mark's, and we decided therefore to make a beeline for Lombok. All night we motored, confident that we couldn't miss such a large island and looking forward to refilling with much needed water.

John Roben , Made Monoh and lunch

# Chapter 5

## Back to Bali

Dawn revealed Mt Rinjani and the Alas Strait well to our left so it was clear Maday and John were intending to keep up the pressure for going back to Bali. John now mentioned that he had entered for an important surfing competition in a few days' time so they were now working on our consciences as well. Harry and Mark were in the vomitorium feeling ill and not caring where they went as long as it was dry land. I suspected John had slipped some poisonous oriental herb into their fried rice in order to produce some acquiesence and rummaged around the fish box to see if there was anything that might have counteracted food poisoning, but the nearest I came to it in that box of esoteric medicaments were some phials of antidote for an Egyptian cobra, an African mamba and a sand viper. On the principle of anything being better than nothing, I diluted some African mamba antidote and gave it to them to swig down and while I was at it gave John and Made a drink of sand viper antidote as they seemed to be enviously eyeing the preparation for Harry and Mark.

When we reached the coastline we found it was steep with a heavy undulating surf and impossible to land the boat. Hunched over the charts again it seemed that Labuan Haji, further east - to the dismay of the crew - was our nearest port, but we sweetened this by declaring that from Labuan Haji we would go back to Bali so that John could join his new role-models in the surfing competition. Labuan Haji was positioned so that it would be easier to return to Bali by continuing all the way round the island so we would have a chance to see the southern, less visited side of the island.

In order to get some fresh water I swam ashore with one empty jerrycan to scout out the territory, and the first thing that struck me was the Mediterranean appearance of the landscape. Burnt grass, dry, buff-coloured hillsides, goats, cows and ponies. I introduced myself to a villager who insisted on my drinking some strong coffee served in small glasses - another Mediterranean touch, and then assisted in getting some brackish water from the village well. All around the village were big healthy coconut trees so the water table was obviously not too deep and reasonably consistent. Back at the foreshore a fisherman kindly stopped mending his nets to ferry me back to the boat in a small sampan.

Tommy was fired up again and while Made and John-Robin slept after their efforts during the night we motored round to Labuan Haji, a small town overlooking the Alas Strait which divides Lombok from Sumbawa. We arrived in the evening at a simple village port dominated by the massive backdrop of Mt Rijani which in the evening light looked purple. As at Reo the actual town was some distance away and the port, if it could be called that, was divided into two sections; the first, a wide sandy beach with a circling coral reef some distance off with a narrow entrance, through which we had come, was suitable for small craft; and an area to the east where anchorage could be obtained in fifteen metres of water where larger craft went. The pilot book mentioned that the town was readily identifiable by the chimney of a rice mill, and we had imagined that there would be many other signs to indicate the largest settlement on the eastern side of the island, but in the event we saw very little and were heading towards what we thought was a village to ask directions when we realised that we had arrived.

As usual none of the boats had engines, all being an assortment of sailing craft, and most being small enough to paddle. There were perhaps a dozen boats there. We stayed on board for the night as it was difficult to see the layout on shore and we were all either tired or feeling seedy.

In the morning Mt Rinjani was covered in early-morning mist while the sandy foreshore was a hive of activity. This was surprising as the only visible building was a white painted godown, obviously something to do with the government, nestling beneath a heavy profusion of coconut trees. There was no sealed area around it or anywhere else, just sand and coconut trees. No dogs either. It was instantly recognisable as a Moslem area. We waded ashore and across the short patch of beach which had been churned up by people searching for bait, and by scores of feet which had come down to the sea in the early morning for one reason or another. Perhaps the most unusual and pleasant aspect, which didn't register immediately, was the complete lack of transport whether mechanised or horse-drawn; people were wandering around on foot only. But as this was a port there had to be something and a little later a few Toyota landcruisers and motorscooters appeared.

In front of the white godown were some 44 gallon oil drums containing fuel, but it was not, as we were soon informed by the inhabitants of the building, for sale; from the godown a sand road, flanked by unbroken clusters of palm trees, led inland.

We got all our empty cans, red for fuel, blue for water, ashore and hired a Toyota landcruiser to take us to town. Sprinkled underneath the palm trees along the way were neat little houses with red tiled roofs and, in what seemed like Dutch influence, picket fences, often painted white, surrounding them. The guide book gave the thumbs down to this town and among other things suggested that tourist accommodation could only be found on a *warung* bench with the owner and his wife sleeping beneath! Perhaps because of the warning we approached the people with circumspection so that nothing untoward happened. We managed to get fuel and water in the easiest operation to date, and given more time I would have liked to have spent a day or two here to confirm whether it really was so awful and to explore the surrounding countryside which had an empty and attractive air to it, but under the psychological momentum being built up by Made and John we got ready for an immediate departure heading south.

Made was starting to return to his old self; he carefully prepared some fishing lines and took care in teasing the line in the water so that very soon we had caught our first fish for many days, a small shark as it happened. The Balinese won't eat shark meat for some reason but Mark, Harry and myself feasted well. However, they can use it as bait and luckily we soon caught a large tuna so that Made and John were now able to indulge themselves, after which they announced jauntily that they wanted to leave shortly after the moon had set at about 4 o'clock in the morning. We were close to Ringgit point and the further south we had travelled from Labuanhaji the more rocky, barren and desolate the shoreline became. Round Ringgit point itself the sea was rough and no doubt affected by the various currents that were confusingly referred to in the pilot book as doing this or that according to the 'moon's passage' and what the moon's declination happened to be at the time. Both matters were beyond our scope and we rested trustingly in the hands of Made and his favouring travelling at night which may of course have had other motives behind it such as being cooler and less likely to be waylaid by us into an attractive but tricky-to-get-at sandy cove.

Dawn revealed the rocky, steep southern coastline which the ocean swell made inaccessible except in small and occasional sandy bays some of which showed signs of temporary settlements. I couldn't see why there weren't more fishing communities along here, I'm sure the Vietnamese would make a better go of it. There were few features in the desolate, brown country behind. Odd groups of monkeys perched on the rocks and appeared to be scavenging for titbits of marine life. On board the scavenging became more enthusiastic the nearer we got to Bali, more lines were trawled off the back and the boat became covered in drying fish releasing an odour which we were now used to.

We spent a night in one of the small bays and found it a good location for night diving. Made was an expert at this and inspired Mark to follow the fanciful notion of arrowing through the water with a knife gripped between his teeth flicking his body out of the way as a shark comes charging in and ripping its belly open with his knife. Made in fact claimed to have done this, and judging from his skill in the water we were not inclined to ridicule it. The spear guns we had brought from England were lethal things that were primed by hauling back a rigid piece of rubber and clipping it behind a trigger which, with the safety catch off, had a mind of its own. They did nevertheless spear several fish. Larry's excursions into the water always looked promising as he strapped every accessory onto his wetsuit but it usually ended in 'fish spotting'. My own efforts were no better and I concentrated on trying to learn to swim more efficiently but without much success. The moon went down at about 3.30 in the morning and once again Made decided to leave about half an hour later.

We sailed to the end of the south coast of Lombok and into the Lombok Strait for a few miles before reaching the forbidding looking island of Nusa Penida. It's mountainous and dry. Low trees and cacti struggle to survive along with a few marsupials and natives. It marks the boundary between Asia and Oceana in a most dramatic way. Similar to Komodo it was used as a penal colony for the kingdom of Klungkung on Bali.

There was a heavy swell all along the coastline which was bounded by high vertical cliffs rising straight out of the sea as at Dover but here they were black as opposed to white. In some places there had been landslips which gave an opportunity for perilous looking sections of bamboo to be lashed together and form a ladder down to where fresh water could be gathered from streams bubbling out of the rock face, and on further to where eggs could be collected from the nesting birds, and on still further to where various sorts of edible marine life could be searched for, but this must have been for the bravest of the brave because the caves and recesses in the rocks were lashed with great geysers of spray and spume and occasional waves were momentarily forced up through the narrow entrances by the swell. I noticed one person who was fishing from some flimsy construction that projected out from a seemingly sheer rock face a 100 feet from the water and 200 feet from the top.

We sailed past the two rocks of Batu Lombong where clouds of fruit bats funnelled out of their summits and flapped around our boat with their vampire-like heads eyeing us questioningly while their screams competed with the surf pounding on the rocks. Thus we arrived at the beautiful and deserted coral island called Ceningan located off the western end of Nusa Penida. It was surrounded by protecting reefs and the limpid waters ranged from cobalt blue to white as one peered down through thirty feet of crystal clear water to the varying things on the seabed. Across a narrow strait was Lembongan island and at the head of an empty bay Made had anchored the boat belonging to 'Philippe,' the Frenchman. It was he who had urged us always to accept whatever Made suggested and in the normal reaction against being given advice by a stranger we felt an illogical antipathy towards Philippe. This feeling may have been increased by Made invariably using 'Oui,oui' whenever an affirmative answer was required which he had obviously picked up from Philippe and which he clearly considered to be the correct answer to give to white men. Little did he know how irritating these two little words could become, and we tried to devise ways in which we could address him without prompting them. After hearing hundreds of repetitions of this word it was hardly surprising to discover that the pidjin English for a Frenchman in the Pacific is 'man oui oui,' while the idiomatic English usage is presumably a sort of feeble protest.

Now we were faced with more provocation. Philippe's boat was called - wait for it - Sri Noa Noa. It was well over forty feet long with a spacious cabin and had been lovingly constructed out of local materials by local craftsmen. As Made watched us looking at the boat and then talking earnestly among ourselves he suddenly began to seem slightly nervous and his proud ebullience started evaporating like the curling tufts of smoke that came out of Tommy at full stretch.

He had every reason to be nervous. What were we doing we wondered in a twenty foot cow transporter with a vomitorium when only Made stood between us and the Sri Noa Noa? Made was in imminent danger of being turned into an Asian Captain Bligh and with native intuition he had quickly latched onto it. His solution was to invite us aboard so that, our curiosity satisfied, we might continue peacefully. His other motive was more cunning because Philippe had apparently asked Made to try and sell it to us, so he was anxious to emphasise its good points. It was certainly impressive with two big masts and an enormous bowsprit. The cabin area was designed with maximum space in mind so that there was ample headroom for a tall person and it was possible to move around passing one another comfortably. Its intention was as much to appeal to somebody cruising the islands as to an intrepid sailor tackling oceans. Like other boats we had seen, it was made in Kalimantan and everything was made out of tropical hardwoods and it had a very nice feel to it despite the dinky little batik curtains.

The price was far too high and our mutinous spirit had worn off so we squashed back onto the *Gin Pahit*, and while the others motored round to Batu Jungu on the north west side to do some diving I was dropped on the shore and headed for the same village, about three miles distance, by walking across the island which has a gentle hill of 320 feet running down the centre of it. Once again there was a Mediterranean feel to the neat little villages with dry-stone walls, carefully tended plots and various animals ranging around. Coconut palms lined small paddy fields where Balinese girls, most of them topless, worked together. There was an air of permanence and antiquity, and perhaps most pleasant of all the people smiled and waved a friendly greeting as I passed by. The good feelings promoted by such simple actions sometimes made me think of its reverse in the surly, dour Moslem villages where you riskes a rock being thrown at you.

At the top of the hill there was a marvellous view across to Bali and Mt Agung and I lingered there a little while before descending down to Batu Jungu, which happened to be Made's home port so that he and John-Robin had wasted no time in joining their relatives to relive the past month and have an impromptu party lasting well into the night, frustrating our intention to do some night-diving. It also started to rain for the first time on our trip so with the boat perched on the beach all we could do was huddle in the vomitorium and wait for our drunken crew to return; this role-reversal continued when they finally did appear at 3 o'clock in the morning in such an abandoned state of inebriation that they declared there was no longer any point in night diving and it would be much better to set off to Bali forthwith. Blearily we accepted the situation and as the tide was coming in fast we were soon afloat and on our way with Made and John conversing noisily in the cockpit.

Early in the morning we arrived off Sanur where hundreds of Balinese were swimming. The tide was right in and there was a heavy swell causing us to surf through the gap in the reef passing close to the wreck. Once the difficult process of unloading all the gear through the surf had been completed, the trip was now over. We hired a *bemo* to take us back to Mark and Harry's house, where the only gadget in the house was a Chinese generator made by the firm of Don Feng; it had long stood idle but Mark, with the confidence of having mended Tommy in a crisis, applied himself to mending it, and presently, after he had been furiously winding the handle of the heavy flywheel, it fired falteringly, causing the handle to kick uncontrollably and jack-knife Mark to one side. Slowly it picked up speed and in contrast to the past month's privations complete comfort was now assured by having a power supply, so while one of the local villagers massaged Mark's sore elbow, we drained the last bottle of John Roben,

Harry holds a shark while Mark gets a surprise removing a fishhook from it's mouth

# Chapter 6

## *Lossman Life and on to Kupang*

I had seen many potentially interesting places on this trip, but nothing that had immediately been 'right'. I hoped now that a land trip followed by going to more remote islands further east in the Nusa Tenggara group, might yield something.

Komodo island may well be a prime development site in the right hands but it was isolated with poor communications and would the dragons, with a taste for living flesh, be a better prospect than the Communist regime in Vietnam? At the time it wasn't appreciated that most of the refugees were economic ones looking for a location with better business opportunities rather than escaping political oppression, so on that basis the islands seen would not have been suitable. It either needed a remote area on one of the larger islands in the Nusa Tenggara group or a bigger island with more rainfall.

Mark and Harry soon returned to London leaving the *Gin Pahit* with Made and John-Robin at my disposal. Not surprisingly Made, having just been reunited with his family and with a pocket full of cash, was not keen to set off again. He did however assure me with completely believable sincerity that he "knew a man that could".

I scoured the Admiralty pilot book but finally settled for Ian Whitton's suggestion of the island of Wetar, north of Timor. It was described as a rugged, mountainous island with the two highest peaks reaching 4,500 feet. It was approximately twenty miles by fifteen miles and only sparsely inhabited along the coast. This was beginning to sound hopeful and as a clincher I read that one of the bays was called Labuan Airpanas - hot-water bay - it had hot springs which could serve as a hot water supply until alternative arrangements were made.

I hurried off to see Made, and find out his progress but he had disappeared, and his wife gave some bland assurances about his reappearance. There now followed a period of evasive behaviour and time wasting promises that very nearly had the effect that he probably wanted them to have - for me to get fed up and go quietly back to London leaving him with the boat and engine.

The crew he had conjured up for me was none other than John-Robin. Obviously I knew from recent experience that he was a pleasant enough youth when describing his surfing experiences but as far as sustained work was concerned he had been fairly useless and even on the principle of the 'devil you know' I was reluctant to take him on again as Made must have known. Furthermore his loyalties would again be to getting the trip over with as quickly as possible.

As we made arrangements, both of us no doubt felt that once under way things could be worked out satisfactorily. One of the compromises arrived at was that John could go straight off to Lembongan, get married and enjoy a nibble of forbidden fruit for a few days, like a young warrior on the eve of a dangerous exploit.

The difficulties of sailing these boats was well demonstrated in a documentary film of a convoy of these boats, crewed by Europeans, sailing from Bali to Darwin

One of the reasons I had persevered in getting a local crew was because local regulations stipulated that an Indonesian registered craft had to have an Indonesian captain, and much time was now spent in bureaucratic hassles trying to work out a way in which, if the mood should take me, I could sail round Timor and to the Torres Strait islands a short distance to the south and belonging to Australia. Every department imaginable had to give its approval and charge its baksheesh. An exception was the police chief, who was the most friendly and helpful of all. He had had some training in America and couldn't understand why the hippies that crowded into Bali forming the largest group of foreigners, were so scarce in America, "I looked everywhere for hippies without seeing one"; and he wanted to get rid of them more because his self-respect was offended that it was the seedy elements of Western society coming to Bali rather than any specific objection to the people themselves.

This conversation prompted me to spend an evening in the hippie quarter of Kuta where I knew by repute there was a whole subculture blending white people speaking a variety of languages, Asian people speaking a variety of languages and the Balinese themselves all doing their best to set the world an example by their alternative lifestyle.

Simple clothing factories and cheap jewellery workshops had sprung up amid the ancient village. Local families who owned enough land had built lodging houses in the form of individual huts called lossmen grouped around a central hut doing service as an office. I shoehorned myself into a pair of skintight jeans, bought a dinky cotton baju and debated whether to go the whole way and hang a trinket round my neck; then I was off into Kuta's urban jungle...

A heavy pall of acrid smoke, each lossman window acting as a trickling tributary, wafted through the coconut palms and across the whole area. A lowly mumble of voices like a religious dirge, occasionally punctuated with a raised "wow man" or just "wow", came into focus and out again as I picked my way along the narrow sandy paths. Also picking their way along the narrow sandy paths were Balinese women of uncertain age carrying rattan baskets, like shopping baskets, inside of which were the tools of their trade, namely various types of Eastern oils including macassar oil from a nearby island of the same name. This was the oil which caused such worry to Victorian hostesses trying to keep the plush on their armchairs untouched from heads coated with it and as a result invented the 'anti-macassar', a lacy cloth draped over the back of the chair which is still retained by people whose acquaintances use Brylcreem grease on their hair.

Here, however, the oils were used to massage the tired limbs of surfers or the tension from neck muscles tautened through wrestling with metaphysical topics. It was also about as close as most male visitors got to any physical contact with the local feminine population. This was in contrast to female tourists where the situation would warm the heart of the most fervent feminist. Every Balinese boy considers it a sacred initiation rite to sleep with as many

Western girls as he can and towards this goal he is assisted by an unending line of Australian secretaries looking for an exotic holiday romance.

Stumbling out of a complex of lossmen called 'Golden Village', which some wag had crossed out and substituted with 'Needle Park' I found myself on a narrow sealed road lined with *warungs* and discos. The first to catch my attention was called the Rum Jungle; judging from the multi-decibel racket of strangled vowels I knew what to expect but curiosity led me to confirm that indeed about fifty fat Australian secretaries and a hundred lithe young Balinese bucks were either conducting shouted conversations above the music or draped over one another on the postage stamp-sized dance floor.

Emerging, and taking care to step off the road every few moments as a whirring motorcycle loaded with beachboy and surfing equipment came speeding recklessly past, I hadn't gone very far before bumping into somebody I had met in one of the offices I had been shuttling between. "Come to a party" she said with great enthusiasm, so back into the palm trees we went and by some skilful navigation arrived at a large lossman on the beach. It's easy to see why the beautiful wide beach at Kuta with its regular surf became so popular and although Australia has many such beautiful beaches they're not 'abroad', and the Aborigines apparently don't have the same appeal for the Australians as the Balinese.

I was on the wrong wavelength for this party and to adapt probably would have required several days chanting "wow" in one of the smoke filled lossmen. First a Robinson Crusoe figure offered round some of the little airline towelettes that are dispensed on planes to 'freshen up'; whether this was a gesture of hospitality, an offer to freshen up, or just getting rid of some merchandise that wasn't selling in his shop, I never discovered. Perhaps it was merely his sense of humour.

Shortly after this I saw a bald headed Spaniard called Manuel, whom I had been talking to quite rationally, put ketchup over his ice cream; moving on, an American solemnly informed me that he had only come to the party from his base in the upland area of Ubud because "I gotta get down to the ocean".

Going onto the beach I joined an emaciated looking figure with a W.G. Grace beard being cross examined by a hippie entrepreneur type, a character that looked as though he could dress up and speak with a capitalist tongue as easily as dressing down and conversing in significant monosyllables. There was some minor dispute between them with the bearded figure as the supplicant; he seemed to be losing the argument so to give himself time to marshal some new thoughts he removed a plastic pouch of Old Holborn rolling tobacco and began constructing a cigarette with bright yellow nicotine-stained fingers topped by thick, long, grime-encrusted fingernails. When he had finished, his protagonist held forward a cigarette lighter in a helpful way but at the last second lowered his hand so that the flame caught the smoker's beard which flared up in a crackle.

"Aaagh!" W.G. Grace flung his cigarette to one side, grabbed his beard and made for the sea to dip his head under water but before reaching the shoreline realised that he had only been scorched and wasn't burning. Before the dispute could gather momentum, I wandered off in the direction of some more loud music further down the beach.

This experience among the lossmen where people's primary aim was to 'communicate' with one another, and thereby form one big happy family is being attempted at a less successful level in forums like the European Community. However, it seems to me that before we attempt to organise a single currency we need a common language. Once people can talk together anything is possible. At present it's the cart before the horse.

I'm always struck that countries with a completely different culture, that are however united by speaking English through being former colonies, open up in a way that is impossible between the UK and Europe, despite its proximity and cultural similarities. Most mainland EC countries teach languages as a priority but in the United Kingdom earnest debates on the national curriculum still fail to address this necessity.

Lack of communication attracts irrational antipathy, suspicion and fear. I remember native people telling me they 'hated' neighbouring tribes because they "spoke another language". Edward Lear, the artist and humorist who lived in San Remo, and was regarded by all who knew or met him as being a benign and helpful person, was treated with hostility when he spent periods virtually incommunicado.

Ridiculously trivial logistical and bureaucratic problems succeeded one another preventing my departure until it all culminated in having everything loaded onto the boat, one hand on the anchor rope ready to pull it up, and John-Robin doing a disappearing act. I had to unload everything again and get it stored, during which time my irritation increased to the point where I felt that when I finally located John-Robin there might be a scene whereby we parted company permanently, so I went to Made and told him I would return in a month and if John-Robin wasn't ready to leave then, he would have to answer for the consequences.

This turn of events wasn't as inconvenient as it might have been as I was planning to go overland through some of the islands after this boat trip, so now I decided to reverse my itinerary; Flores in particular had been mentioned as having a sparsely inhabited interior but with the benefit of a reasonable infrastructure on the coast, and I got a similar impression from the local people I had spoken to in Reo. I decided to go by way of Kupang in West Timor, because my attempts at finding out whether it was possible to visit East Timor, where a war was in progress, and close to Wetar island where I wanted to get to, had been inconclusive. Certainly nobody had been prepared to sell me a ticket there or grant any sort of permission.

The flight to Kupang took one hour and we flew over Sumba. Of the ten passengers four of them were soldiers rejoining their units. The landscape was hot and scorched, the people were predominantly negroid in appearance and in general very friendly. There was none of the customary hustling, in fact they were subdued and helpful to the extent of offering lifts and information if they thought you needed it.

I went to the Hotel Flobamor where I met a couple of Australians who had arrived from Broome in their own plane. They knew Timor well and had been in Dili in 1975 when the war between this former Portuguese colony and Indonesia had started.

The Portuguese had been in East Timor since the sixteenth century but were challenged by the Dutch who set up a trading station in Kupang, West Timor, in the seventeenth century. For a hundred years skirmishes took place until the Dutch, who had been getting the worst of it, turned their attention to other islands in the enormous archipelago. An uneasy status quo remained until the Japanese invasion in 1942, the subsequent Javanese colonisation and creation of the Indonesian state in 1947 encompassing most of the Dutch territories in the East Indies. Timor thus survived as a small independent Portuguese territory surrounded by a hostile Indonesia until 1975 when Indonesia, on the pretext of forestalling the possibility of a 'Cuba' on its doorstep, invaded, and ever since an under-reported war has been in progress.

Captain Bligh, and his loyal crewmen, arrived here in 1791 after their long row from Tonga following the mutiny on the Bounty. In the nineteenth century it was used by English and American whalers. Despite this popularity with Europeans over several centuries it hasn't developed any industries or much else. There were no buildings over thirty feet, street lighting hadn't been installed very long. It must have looked very similar when Captain Bligh entered the huge sweeping bay with the scrub covered mountains behind and palm trees sheltering simply constructed dwellings along the foreshore.

I arrived on a Sunday to the sound of church bells, and this reflected the predominantly Christian population drawn not only from local islands but from the many sailors, traders and passengers who had arrived over the years so that every racial type was represented. Naturally it was also a melting pot that had produced a pleasantly lackadaisical population of coffee coloured people, as opposed to the vigour sometimes attributed to the mixing of blood.

The absence of employment opportunities - most people compete to become government clerks, join the police or army or hospital staff - meant the hotels had a surplus of willing labour for the few tourists that came through. At the Flobamor, putting a wet towel down for an instant produced a reflex action from a member of staff called Hansi who sprang at it like a terrier at a bolting rat and hung it up to dry. Outside the hotel, a local youth called 'Feri' sat in a jeep with a union jack embossed on the back of one wing mirror and the stars and stripes on the other, ready to drive anybody 'off road' for little more than the cost of the petrol; furthermore his command of English enabled me to arrange my passage up to Ende on the south coast of Flores with relative ease. We had gone down to Kupang's port at Tanau where various Buginese craft were loading or unloading and found one going to Flores and then when I had taken a deep breath preparatory to negotiating the fare and facilities, Feri had spotted the ensuing storm and weighed into the supercilious-looking pirates until a satisfactory bargain had been struck. While this was going on I was fascinated by the complex manoeuvring of the various craft, relying on sampans to constantly raise and reposition anchors.

On shore I spotted a group of girls pounding coffee beans in the same way I seen them doing at the factory where I had gone to look at an outboard engine in Surabaya for the *Gin Pahit*; the building was so ancient-looking with huge thick walls, and small windows that I was inspired to enquire its history. Feri seemed a bit nonplussed but diligently translated my questions to the girls. When it became clear to me that I was getting nowhere, and to the girls that I wasn't trying to be funny, and to Feri that we were all at cross-purposes, he gently explained that we were at the ancient old brothel. No doubt Captain Bligh's men paid it a visit while they waited for a boat back to Europe. Like the rest of the town, it had an unassuming air and the prefabricated extension being built at the back I imagine was in belated response to the thousands of soldiers stationed in Kupang for operations in East Timor.

Back at the hotel I was about to take a siesta in accordance with Portuguese inspired local tradition when a soldier knocked on the door and asked if he could borrow a razor. He had just arrived from Dili where such items were unobtainable; it reminded me of an Indian who told me that he considered the only worthy contribution the British had made to India during their administration was the razor blade. I lent him the razor and in return heard some of his stories of the operations in East Timor. He himself was engaged in directing artillery fire from a hovering helicopter although more people were surrendering from starvation due to the rains failing than from army activity. He also claimed, unprompted, that it was 'communists' who had killed three Australian journalists and two British ones; the facts were quite different and I could only assume the impending use of my razor made him anxious not to offend.

The next morning, loaded with my baggage, I skirted past Hansi to avoid him springing forward to insist on doing all sorts of unnecessary things and outside to where Feri was dozing in his jeep with his indispensable mirror sunglasses anchored to his face with springy wire clasps curling round his ears; his mouth was open and flies were buzzing around it. I debated whether to leave him in comfortable slumber but his reason for being there were the modest fares, so I opened the door and swung my bag in. He blinked awake, lubricated his dry mouth and reset his ingratiating smile, "Tanau?" he asked.

"Yes" I answered, and we rumbled off down the potholed road. I was expecting confusion at the port, and I got it, so I was able to remain unruffled throughout the last minute 'procedures'. The captain of the boat asked for my 'papers'; he probably assumed that I wouldn't have any and would then quote him from the previous day when he said I didn't need any, whereupon he would reply with mock regret he had been mistaken, but that it could all be cleared up with a little baksheesh.

However, I was half expecting this and confidently produced one of the documents referring to the *Gin Pahit* which was smothered in an impressive array of Indonesian official rubber stamps. He wasn't able to read and importantly turned the piece of paper this way and that, nodding at the different rubber stamps, and shortly before he could demand another piece of paper to pretend he knew what it all meant and have a final go at extracting money, I flourished my international driving licence at him, which is likewise covered in fancy looking print, and has the great distinction of having several different scripts not to mention one's photograph. As a standby in these situations it rarely fails and has the great advantage of having to be renewed at least once a year so it always appears as an up to date document.

The pirate looked at it and nodded at me as if to say "that was the one I wanted to see". I now bid adieu to Feri and stored my case below.

I returned to the deck to watch the final loading up of drums of kerosene for delivery to Ende. Kerosene is lighter than water so the 44 gallon drums were floated out to the boat in a long file, like short fat logs. Winching them aboard and stowing them was hard work, and by the time it was done the smell of kerosene was overpowering while below it was asphyxiating, but the hot weather would have prevented me from spending much time below anyway.

The loading of the boat provided the right opportunity to familiarise myself with the crew and gain a superficial impression of what they were like. Most people are supposed to be 'wonderful' when you 'get to know them', but often the first contact with them doesn't produce the inclination to want to do that, even if there was time, so I hoped to glean who was likely to be an ally and who not.

Inevitably 'characters' emerged, the first was a ragged fellow, practically useless and often the butt of the other crewmen's jokes. They described him as an Indonesian tourist from Komodo, and his nickname was 'Black Beauty'.

The tide began to turn indicating that our departure was imminent, but before pulling up the anchors, they prostrated themselves in correct Moslem fashion towards Mecca. I was somewhat relieved to see them strictly observing their religious tenets because I had packed a bottle of booze for the trip, and I had wondered how long it would last among a thirsty crew. So I duly informed the captain that, as a Christian, I didn't want to be responsible for encouraging practices that contravened their Moslem faith and therefore I would not be offering them anything to drink. He gave me the same sort of look that he had given when I first produced a 'paper' in response to his request for 'papers', and he said "We drink normally". I couldn't think of an effective response to that and feebly replied "Really", and wandered down the deck nursing my whisky and soda. However, conscience got the better of me and I unpacked a box of stale Sumatran cigars left over from the recent *Gin Pahit* trip, and distributed them, much to their satisfaction.

As a crew, as opposed to individually, they were dirty, demanding and loud, and took it in turns to ask the same questions and make the same requests. The captain was treated with slight deference so by sitting in his vicinity I could avoid for a time the facetious banter of the crew.

Most of these old macassar schooners have something major that needs replacing, and in this case it was the rudder. Until such time as it could be done two temporary rudders had been lashed to the sides in the same configuration as the *Gin Pahit.* Surprisingly the system was quite robust. The boat had been made in the Bone Rate islands which was the group that we had been heading for when we sailed north from Reo, and I felt a touch of nostalgia when he told me the engine came from Surabaya.

They had been to Australia twice; I didn't enquire where, but I imagine it was to fish in some of the reefs or visit the Torres Strait islands. The only large town nearby would have been Darwin and I doubt whether they would have gone there for anything. Perhaps they had gone pearl-poaching near Broome.

In the evening the captain and I had our food on his private poop deck while behind, on another poop deck shielded by a plank of wood eighteen inches high, the crew could relieve themselves using sand as lavatory paper so that following their performance they sounded like a cat scratching in its litter-tray. Later I spread myself out on a convenient part of the deck and went gently off to sleep.

Although we sailed for part of the time the winds and currents were not helpful, and we motored much of the way. Early in the morning a large whale floating placidly nearby provided a nice sight.

Presently, on the horizon a mountain appeared and then another and another, which became larger and larger the closer we got. Eventually we reached the coast, with the rugged mountains behind smouldering and smoking in different places, giving the impression that they were about to erupt at any moment.

The town and port of Ende, like many other similar ports and towns, is at the mouth of a large inlet, and in this case overpowering volcanic mountains loom behind puffing out smoke as a warning and a reminder of nature's powerful position in the grand order of things. One volcano close to the town had at some recent time completely blown its top out, and black volcanic sand lined the steeply dipping shore; it was clear that the sides of the mountains continued for hundreds if not thousands of feet to the seabed.

Simple fishermen's houses with thatched roofs and brightly painted walls mingled with the equally brightly painted boats along the shore, and the sun's rays enhanced the intensity of the contrast between the bright colours sandwiched between the dull blue of the sea, the black sand and the brown mountains.

Taking leave in Ende harbour, south Flores Island, after sailing from Kupang in Timor

# Chapter 7

## *Walking across Flores*

I went ashore with the captain in the boat's little sampan, past an Australian yacht with six people aboard. I spoke to them briefly as we passed and they seemed short tempered in the way that happens to yacht crews cooped up at close quarters for long periods.

The captain had a house in Ende, and his family provided a small celebration for our safe arrival. A crewman was then designated to carry my bags to a lossman. I was wearing a solar topi and carrying a rolled umbrella, which prompted some passers-by to tease my porter for being a 'Dutchman's lackey', and others to smile and give a thumbs up sign. I was careful, however, not to get too short with anybody because there is a fighting system in Indonesia, where the combatants use sticks, whips and shields to beat the living daylights out of one another. I tentatively asked my porter if he knew about it. "Yes of course," he said, "it was developed here and is still popular."

My lossman was the usual flea-ridden, dirty, noisy, bedraggled affair, but it had a marvellous view of the mountains. No doubt Sukarno had taken similar inspiration when he was exiled here by the Dutch in the 1930s. His house is still preserved on the outskirts of the town.

I spotted the crew of the Australian yacht grimly walking along avoiding talking to one another, and no doubt dealing with the bureaucratic niceties that I was familiar with from the *Gin Pahit*.

Flores is reputed to be a beautiful island with rolling tropical forests in the east and interior, and smoking volcanos dotted across the centre. The inland people are Roman Catholic with a long history of musical and cultural diversity; they are also better disposed towards Westerners than the Moslems along the coast. This persuaded me to aim at an overland trip to Maumere in the north of the island.

In order to make a decisive start I decided to take a bus in the direction of the three famous volcanic lakes at Kelimutu near Moni, approximately fifty kilometres from Ende. Four hours after the bus's scheduled departure time we were still stationary in the bus station, the half dozen passengers not being enough apparently for the driver to set off. I then read in the guide book that the Flores buses leave 'this year, next year, sometime, never'. I went off to hire a bemo.

A negotiation took place and I climbed into the front and off we went. Big mountain ranges loomed up in front as we sped past plunging river valleys and subtropical vegetation. The rainfall is erratic, caused probably by excessive forest-clearing. Agriculture was widespread in the sparse landscape, while domestic animals were left to forage for themselves in the forest covering the tops of the hills.

The island has seen waves of migrations pass through and Hindu relics jostle with ancient musical instruments found only in the Balkans while some of the carvings show resemblances to those on Easter Island.

There were many fires burning which I assumed was part of the process of clearing the hillsides prior to planting. The people were curly headed Melanesian types, generally dense-looking and chewing betel nut. There is one particularly vacuous expression that I think might reflect excessive anaemia caused by hookworm. No doubt other debilitating parasites were at work as well.

Imperceptibly however, the scenery, both geographically and ethnographically, improved the further we went - more forest cover and the odd friendly wave. I asked the driver to stop at a roadside stall for a drink, and walking past the back of the bemo was surprised to see the half-dozen bus passengers from Ende sitting there.

"What are you doing?" I asked. No answer of course, so I ordered them out. That didn't work so I tackled the driver who suddenly had difficulty understanding me.

"Well at least tell me where they are going" I finally asked.

"Just up the road," he replied. So off we went again. We soon reached the turn-off point for the lakes which were another thirteen kilometres up a steep track, along which were no villages. I looked enquiringly at the driver and then at the back of the bemo. He shrugged his shoulders, and continued driving.

About a kilometre from the lakes the road was barred by a single bamboo pole and an Indonesian clutching some cloakroom tickets. It was in the middle of nowhere, with no 'booth' or printed notice to suggest it was official. The toll man looked at us, and then shuffled to the back of the bemo, returned, and counted out eight grubby, crumpled, already detached, cloakroom tickets.

"That will be 8,000 rupiah" he said.

"I'm not paying for the passengers," I replied, "tell them to get out and wait, we'll pick them up on the way down." The dense looking 'bus passengers' sat there looking dense, while the driver and toll man became similarly uncooperative.

An uneasy thought began to niggle that something like this happens on a regular basis. I peeled off 8,000 rupiahs and we drove up to the lakes. Tourist literature had described these close-together lakes nestling in a volcanic crater as being bright blue, red and green. On this day, one was dull turquoise, another muddy maroon and the other grey, suggesting a lot of volcanic sediment. I paced around the area admiring the scenery while garish music blasted out of the bemo. The six 'bus passengers' had metamorphosed into sightseers and were enthusiastically discussing the lakes. It was now clear that I had provided them with a day out. Later I expect they shared the 8,000 rupiahs, and returned in the evening to tell their children stories of the wild and dangerous hinterland and buy their wives a box of chocolates. What else are overseas tourists for?

Kelimutu Lake, Flores Island

We were at an altitude of 1,690 metres and the sea was clearly visible. We were soon back in the bemo rattling down to Moni. Here I said goodbye to my bemo and watched it disappear back towards Ende with the six passengers still in the back.

The guide book mentioned that the best place to stay was with the Catholic mission, but I thought this 'tip' would not be appreciated by the mission itself, and set off to find something else. However, the locals soon indicated that the mission was the correct place to stay, and so I headed towards the priest's house. The church had been consecrated in 1958 and still looked new. The priest was a local, and most welcoming. He supervised me totally, down to telling me to comb my hair. Then he organised some food which he thought I would find palatable. The first course was bread; this was followed by potatos, and then margarine. He knew that the three ingredients were eaten by white people, but didn't realise that the margarine went on the bread. He sat watching and making comments throughout the 'meal', delighted that I appreciated his efforts. After this I produced brandy and cigars and we got down to discussing my proposed trip. He hadn't heard of anybody wanting to walk from here to Maumere, but thought that it should be possible, but he warned me that some of the mountains were very steep.

The following morning Fr Louis Lada led me through an eccentric breakfast (after I had combed my hair - he must have been told to do this when he was training), and then took me to an 'Adat' village nearby. This was still pagan and contained many intricate carvings; there were sites for animist rituals and carved wooden figures dressed up in beautifully woven clothes to act as talismen. On the outskirts of the village were stone pillars ready to receive offerings to the gods. There were also stones in the main room of the village representing peace treaties.

Fr Louis organised a boy and a pony. The luggage, the pony and myself were tried in all different combinations, but it was eventually settled that the baggage would go on the pony and I would walk. The pony was very sure footed on the steep narrow paths. It was the dry season with the rivers dried up, although the cultivated fields in the valleys below us were a patchwork of different shades of green. The farming techniques were well developed and the land looked fertile. Dry stone walls divided fields and property. There were more fires in the distance burning the thick high grass of fields that had been lying fallow.

There were more grubby negroid people chewing betel nut. The women carried things on their heads, and when not doing this piled up their hair and stuck combs in it resembling miniature garden forks. A.R. Wallace also comments on the necessity to use miniature garden forks with their wire type hair:

"Their frizzly hair is tied in a bunch at the back of the head. They delight in combing, or rather forking it, using for that purpose a large wooden fork with four diverging prongs, which answers the purpose of separating and arranging the long tangled, frizzly mass of cranial vegetation much better than any comb could do."

We arrived at Kerisilo, where I transferred the baggage onto a strong youth. Fr Lada hadn't exaggerated about the hills, and I was soon very tired. Whenever we encountered children they threw down whatever they were carrying and raced away. I wondered what sort of myths had been spun around the whiteman for them to react in this way. We arrived at Pau Bewar village, perched on a promontory, in the early afternoon, and I was unable to go any further. Here I was referred to as 'Tourist' rather than Whiteman, despite them claiming that I was their first tourist. I suspect that the government, in its bid to promote tourism, had informed villages to be on the lookout for wandering white tourists, and that they were coming for their (the villagers') benefit, in the same way that a new hydroelectrical project might be touted. It may also explain the children's behaviour - they were rushing off enthusiastically to pass on the glad tidings of the rare sighting of a 'tourist'.

Moni, Flores

Moni, Flores

Once I had been thoroughly inspected I was put in a storeroom to have a rest. Later I was roused to attend a meeting. The headman looked grim. I handed him my note from Fr Lada requesting that they help me; he read it solemnly.

"This is very heavy baggage, a very dangerous trip. At least two people must go with you, minimum wages of 20,000 rupiahs per day."

"I would like to take six guides and pay them double what you're asking, but I'm afraid it's one man at 10,000 rupiahs per day," I replied.

Their response was to put me back in the storeroom where some voracious bedbugs appreciated my company until the morning.

I was greeted at 5.00 in the morning by a small, wiry, elderly man who had obviously volunteered to do the task at the price I was offering. I strapped my luggage onto him, like a pony, and he visibly sagged. Then away we went into the chilly mountain dawn.

Up and down we went on a rocky, dry path following a river valley with superb scenery. We passed through villages that obviously hadn't received the message about tourism, and the people seemed unnaturally apprehensive. On my own I wouldn't have been able to arrange guides or assistance in them. It was a contrast to somewhere like Borneo where all village folk are approachable.

Several times the path veered off in an unlikely direction and it became clear we were following contours. After about 10.00 in the morning it was so hot that my guide's feet started to burn; he was barefoot, and the rocks were like oven rings. At one time this area must have all been jungle-covered, and where we walked would have been delightfully cool. Now all the hills are stripped, with shades of green where it's grass and scrub, and black where burnt. The people were hard at work clearing and burning prior to planting. The streams coming through the volcanic rocks had picked up some mineral influences which stung the back of my throat when I drank the water. In one stream with a reddish tinge, my guide stopped me from having a drink. There were also extensive encrusted deposits of a white compound over the rocks.

We met hunters out with bows and arrows off to scour the jungle covered hills. The remaining patches of jungle show what an impressive forest it must have been, the volcanic fertility contributing both to its lushness and its demise because farmers appreciate its rich soils.

We went past or through Tanah Mitay, Fatan Dopo, and Detuara where isolated in a nearby valley a huge concrete church had been built. Browns and greens blended together, but the overriding impression was one of a burnt landscape, denuded of forest cover. The individual houses were thatched with long grass and the walls and floors were split bamboo. Most of these communities were in the process of being evangelised by local Roman Catholics. Some remained animist, and were distinguishable by their compactness and the high roofed meeting house in the middle surrounded by stone and bone artifacts. They were also more friendly, waving and shouting from a distance. A barrier of bamboo marked the perimeters of the villages.

Stony paths wove round the mountains giving a magnificent, Mediterranean view. A type of weed six to seven feet high covered the old paddy and had a white flower smelling of honey. Competing with it was a dense foot-high scrub with unscented blue flowers.

We rested at midday because the ground had become too hot for my guide's bare feet. As it was he had to jog along, and the effort stopped him from talking. He wore my solar topi, carried my rucksack with an umbrella sticking out of the top and had a sarong wrapped round his waist.

Our destination that day was Sokonaja village which we could see in the distance, but it was a roundabout route to get there, and we passed the villages of Detunaka, Detudenu, lokoarju, Serosipi and Tanda'au before reaching it. We washed the dust and grime off ourselves in a small river shortly before reaching the village.

The village was barren, just a few crude dwellings dotted about a wide flat open space covered in dried, cracked mud. It must have been ankle deep in mud when it rained. It had the air and appearance of complete apathy. The only sign of life came when I asked if I could take some photographs and they became visibly apprehensive. The unhealthy looking villagers kept up a barrage of hawking, sniffing and spitting. The silhouettes of a few dead trees were the only sign of 'vegetation' apart from some clumps of bamboo.

One of my guides

A ship's lawyer-type appeared called Francis, and was anxious to point out that the village was Roman Catholic. He asked to see my passport, and pretended to the open mouthed villagers surrounding us that it said I was also a Roman Catholic. Despite this erroneous information the villagers didn't unbend very much. A fat Indian-looking man with grey hair, and a protruding lower jaw from which the bottom lip hung slackly revealing a few chipped, stained teeth like rusty railings, gaped inanely as I took a photograph of some nearby goats and pigs. "They're not frightened of the camera," I said to him, "Why are you?" He shuffled forward, enveloped in a voluminous wollen jerkin with two thin legs sticking out of the bottom and said "I don't know."

In the morning a strong wind was blowing clouds of dust between the bamboo slats of the hut. Bamboo was used very extensively, but was obviously going to be in short supply in the near future because soon after leaving the village I passed groves of bamboo which were all dying having just flowered for the first time in decades. I had made an early start in the teeth of a biting wind, leaving the man in a wollen poncho playing cards with a light skinned, green eyed friend while Francis was giving injections to some screaming children.

We made our way downhill following a wide river-bed through some handsome jungle with large trees. Only a trickle of water was flowing through what had the potential to be a roaring torrent. We were joined by a man with elephantiasis. The disease had started near his ankles and was just moving above his knees. Many of the villagers had it, and they claimed it was caused from the urine of a small mud-dwelling creature resembling a newt with a forked tail like a snake's tongue. They rejected the idea that it came from a mosquito bite. They said it took a very long time to move up to the crotch. Sometimes the swelling started in the arms first.

The villages we passed through were Ndokodobay, Detuhowu, Nua Baru, Ndetundura, Ledandori, Lokolandi and then Kota Baru. We were now very close to the coast and the walk had taken much less time than I had expected. The village had coconuts, bananas and a comfortable house to stay in, but the people, while being more friendly, set up a vigil to study every detail about me and what I did. The most routine actions like lifting my wrist to check the time prompted excited discussion.

In the evening there was a 'Recepsi' to celebrate a family moving to Moni. The family, the local police constable and myself sat behind a table on which a large wicker basket had been placed. Guests then arrived, shook hands with each of us, deposited a gift into the basket and sat in rows opposite us. At about 9.00 some serious feasting started with large quantities of arak washing down the food. A dance started with songs such as 'Daylight comes and I wanna go home' blasting through the palms. The constable constantly had drinks pressed on him as villagers sought to ingratiate themselves, and he rapidly entered a state where he became a threat to law and order rather than vice versa, so I felt it a prudent moment to retire and keep an eye on my luggage. My host was a carpenter, and had built himself a superior house, in which I passed a comfortable night.

In the morning there were still a large number of villagers who needed to inspect me further, which fortunately made it easier to get the services of a pony and guide. My original guide had left me here. He had proved to be efficient, reliable and pleasant, so I was happy to donate him my solar topi and umbrella to which he had become very attached. They seemed to put a spring in his step as he departed into the distance. What he really needed, however, was a pair of shoes to protect his feet from the burning sand.

Like the pied piper, I led a column of villagers in the direction of the coast from where it was possible to get a boat to Maumere further along the coast. No boats were going that day of course so we continued on to the village of To-u. Here I stayed in a tree house, the first time I had ever seen such a construction, and it proved a great success. It was cool, clean, away from the dinginess of the huts and oppressiveness of people crowding around. Instead they formed a ring round the base of the tree and stared silently up at it. Occasionally I emerged to give a royal wave and then disappeared again. Later I realised it was protection against tidal waves, and I wondered if it had been high enough when the 1992 wave came through killing over 7,000 people in the surrounding villages. It was at the head of a beach forming part of a wide bay with a beautiful view. It was a fishing village, and needed to be because the burnt hills behind looked barren.

Many more people here had elephantiasis, and I vaguely hoped that my breezy tree house might be protection against the particular mosquito that carries the virus.

My forced stay gave me a familiarity that prompted a stream of questions. "How many years you already stay in Indonesia?" asked one. "Oh about twenty, living all that time in a cave in the hills," I joked. They found this completely plausible, which not only raised the question of how I must have appeared to them, but tempted me to continue, "I've come down to look for a woman to take back with me." They immediately became very sympathetic and concerned, concluding that a light coloured one living in Maumere would be ideal. I felt like a medieval monarch trying to assess the hyperbole before setting forth to inspect the goods personally.

To-u village, Flores

# Chapter 8

## *Back to Bali via the Celebes*

The boat arrived at 6.00 the following morning, and a crush of copra and passengers distributed themselves over it. I found myself comfortably padded by quantities of elephantiasis flesh.

The sea was calm, and the weather and view pleasant so I arrived in Maumere in good shape. The town is predominately Christian so there was no shouting and hustling from the local populace. I was shown to a lossman where an eccentric transvestite rushed about in great excitement arranging everything. S/he was called Sarji and kept the place spotless. There weren't any other guests and my suspicions were soon confirmed when Sarji endeavoured to extend his services in the room.

I fancied I could hear the cackles of some of the boat passengers who no doubt had hoped to see me heading for my cave in the hills with Sarji. Sarji, however, was not to be put off easily. Within an hour of my arrival he had told me his life story, the difficulty he had in choosing the right make-up, physically assaulted me, and pleaded to be helped to have a sex-change operation. After he left my room I heard him having a row with an apparently female voice, followed by him bursting into tears. He then insisted, with make-up and tears streaming down his face, on telling me about the argument.

Despite my sympathy for Sarji's predicament his tiresome attention prompted me to move to the 'Sea World' lossman which was run by an Italian woman called Colletta. I explained my experience in slightly jocular terms, but she hardly reacted. Her partner then appeared, who was a very limp-wristed Italian male, and I suddenly realised that I had leapt out of the frying pan into the fire.

My third attempt was a grumpy, fat Chinese towkay who was obviously used to receiving harassed patrons from the above establishments and set his prices accordingly.

These time wasting incidents are part of the process of travel and tourism. However, how convenient it would be if one could be put on notice that one is entering a zone of hassle, and that it could all be avoided in advance by the payment of a suitable tariff if one is not in the mood to go through it!

My plan was to sail along this coast later, so I was interested to get an idea what sort of boats were for sale and for how much in case the arrangement with the *Gin Pahit* fell through. There is a tradition of boat building in this area, and wooden boats up to 400 tons were being built. Several were ideal and I was close to buying one, and thereby regaining control over my direction of travel. In these countries one's freedom of movement is totally constrained and dependent on what transport is possible or available.

However I resisted an impulse purchase and embraced the familiar hassle and chaos: the Merpati airline office said their weekly plane was cancelled for 'inspeksi', the Pulau Kelapa boat was due to leave for Surabaya, but the engine had to come out and it would take at least a week; the buses to Larantuka and Ende had the same sort of people sitting on them that I had encountered when I arrived in Ende. During this toing and froing I walked past Sarji's lossman and saw him immaculately made-up, trying to coil up the plastic rope used as springs on the metal chairs; he had set his brain a chinese puzzle-type task while he waited for his next victim.

I tried the docks again, and discovered that a large freighter, the KM Nene Mallomo, was on the point of leaving for Ujung Pandang in the Celebes. I raced back to pick up my luggage, and boarded with minutes to spare. The deck doubled as a farmyard, giving us fresh food. The crew was of mixed race and religion, but the captain was Christian so a noisy pig was part of the cargo until it became part of the evening meal, the Moslems naturally enough keeping well clear of the whole business. The divisions in a culturally diverse country like Indonesia are much more rigid on religious grounds than racial ones. Harry from Ambon, working as a deckhand, whose father had converted to Christianity from Islam, seemed more comfortable in my company than with his own race, culture and language.

I woke in the morning off Kalau and the Bone Rate islands. The weather was good, the sea calm and my breakfast was a bowl of chicken stew - the cook having wrung the chicken's neck at dawn. He came from 'Tanah Toraja' and was keen to promote its touristical potential, in part by saying that hundreds of tourists went there. The rest of the crew were clearing cement dust out of the hold. It billowed out in great clouds, and must have been hellish.

Early the following morning we arrived at the 'Semen (the Indonesian translation of cement) Terminal' sixty-five kilometres north of Ujung Pandang. After a lot of manoeuvring we tied up alongside Andi Pangangan of the same line. The whole area was enveloped in cement dust, and the wharf lavatory was a hideous mound of faeces and powdered cement, some of which had set rock hard. Back on board the bureaucrats were confused over my papers. I had given them my permit to sail to Darwin on the *Gin Pahit*, and this now meant that the 'Semen securite' wanted to interview me. "We have procedures here" I was told, and I mentally prepared for a long delay. The bemo which was to take us to the town via the police office arrived and everybody squeezed in, including mountains of fruit, baggage, pigs and chickens.

The captain very kindly volunteered to help me through the procedures and the overloaded bemo halted at the gates where the police office was and in we all went. The crewman from the Moluccas had something to say, then Harry from Ambon and so on through the whole crew. Finally it was my turn: "Indonesian polisi good?" they asked "Very, very good" I replied. "Indonesian securite good?"

"Oh yes," I assured them, and that was the end of the questioning.

We squeezed back into the bemo and set off for Ujung Pandang. Half our livestock died on the journey, but this didn't seem to worry the crew, and the first thing the captain did was to arrange drinks in his house. Harry was then designated to find accommodation for me. I wanted to unwind in a lossman, but he was keen for me to stay with a family living in a large house in the middle of the town. The reason for this turned out to be because they wanted to practice their English and talk about trips they had done to America and Europe. My host was keen that I should have a good impression of Indonesia. and when my becak (a sort of open cabin attached to a scooter) driver returned me to the house and insisted on an inflated fare, he laid him out with swift punch. I think this drastic remedy had been inspired by a boxing world title fight which had been broadcast live that day, and which every office, government included, had watched.

In every Third World country some sort of a festival takes place most days, but on my second day the important 'Pancasila Garuda' was being celebrated. This incorporates the five principles on which the State of Indonesia is founded, a sort of Bill of Rights, and every educated Indonesian is proud to explain it to outsiders.

First you must follow a recognised religion. This was aimed against Communism. Secondly, nationalism: everybody should unite in order to prosper. Thirdly, democracy - as defined in Indonesia, which is based on community discussions leading to decisions. Forthly, humanitarianism in the sense of international cooperation; and lastly, social justice.

It was an appropriate celebration for my host's outlook on life, and I warmly congratulated him on his country's progressive stance.

My pleasant stay in Unjung Pandang had a satisfactory conclusion in a trouble-free flight booking and departure to Bali where I looked forward to my meeting with Made Monoh and John-Robin with anticipation.

# Chapter 9

## *The Gin Pahit Sails Again*

I arrived in Sanur and was pleased to see that, not only were Made and John there, but that they were keen to cooperate. The cooling off period appeared to have been beneficial.

I then made a quick trip to Singapore to buy some spare parts and supplies not available in Bali. While there I recognised many of the long term residents of Bali, also doing their specialist shopping in Singapore.

Back in Bali, I found that contrary to all assurances the engine, which was supposed to be being serviced in Denpasar wasn't ready. More importantly however was the trail of paperwork that needed to be sorted out before departure. About six different authorities have to affix their rubber stamp, and each one has its own form of delay. However, the moment had come to get going and as nothing is ever completely ready I decided to set off without further delay.

I collected several plastic drums of petrol, the unserviced engine, and several boxes of supplies, and went to Sanur. The inevitable last minute change of plan was that John-Robin alone was coming with me, and now suddenly faced with imminent departure, was starting to play up. However, Made chivvied him onto the boat where he became another piece of baggage to be dealt with instead of being useful himself. Before he could jump out I started the engine and we set off for Padang Bai, a small town further round the coast. This stop proved to be very necessary as all the local supplies such as food, lamps, buckets, rope, etc. had been left behind in the confusion of getting John-Robin on board. It was a bad beginning. I bought new supplies and we set off in the evening to sail across the Lombok trough. It was very breezy and we made excellent progress. In the early hours of the morning we spotted a flare to the south-east of us, but there was nothing we could do, even if it had been a genuine distress signal. By dawn we sighted Trewangan island which had obviously had some rain as it was greener than before.

At midday we reached Kampong Anyar on Lombok, which we had visited before, bought some more supplies, and then had a sleep. Again the best wind sprang up in the evening and we set off eastwards. John had decided to sigh loudly at any irritation, and ask repeatedly how long we were going to be away, exactly where we were going and so on.

We were making reasonable progress across the Alas Strait when the engine stopped. It started, but as soon as it was put in gear it stopped, so up went the sail. For two hours at dawn and two hours at dusk, when the wind was changing from onshore to offshore, there would be a lull, and I hoped to use the engine during this time.

Around nine in the morning there was enough breeze to sail along and we went south of Pulau Moyo. It was edged with beautiful looking beaches giving onto some thick woods waiting like a plump cherry waits for Billy Bunter, for the loggers to arrive. John, for a reason known only to himself, wanted to turn round and go south-west to Labuan Haji on the east coast of Lombok. I decided to keep going and we arrived at Pulau Satonda in the evening. With the engine not working we were dependent on the wind's whims, and it quickly dominated not only one's thoughts but one's life. I was reminded of a description of somebody trying to sail from Brunei to Singapore and spending about two months in the process, the wind would blow steadily in the right direction for a couple of days, then it would die and they would drift backwards for several days. This happened several times down the coast of Borneo; they were in sight of Singapore at one point, but again the wind died and it was a few more weeks before they could reach it.

A trickle of wind got us off Satonda island, and we anchored for the night. I also carried out some rudimentary engine maintenance, cleaning some of the obvious parts. For the moment it did the trick.

John had been brooding during this process, and as the engine roared into life his spirits appeared to sink. "I got married two days before we set off," he suddenly announced, clearly implying that he couldn't leave his new bride for too long. Here was an example of reality and fantasy blending; truth was what he wanted it to be, so there was no point in my questioning his veracity by Western standards. I subsequently discovered that he might have got married shortly before setting off, but again, not in the Western sense.

The next morning he seemed to have settled down a bit, apparently less frustrated by the variable winds, saying he was looking forward to reaching Bima, and that he was sure his wife would be pregnant when he returned. However by the afternoon he was getting restless again and was calling on the spirits with more animation than usual. He placed a forest of joss sticks around the boat, alternately moaning and trilling. One noise, designed to discipline the wind was a high-pitched rolling of 'r's, similar to a beater trying to flush out pheasants. We pushed well north of Satonda island, but then as the currents and winds got to work we came floating back off the Sumbawa coast, and giving up the struggle for the day anchored at Kawinda Nae village, Sanggar. The headman produced a bottle of honey from the hills, and some coconuts. John wasn't interested, he had got used to a diet of white rice and catsup which possibly explained his erratic behaviour. Also on the beach were about twenty villagers intently playing gongs; even our arrival didn't break their concentration. They were acting as though they were in the middle of a religious ceremony, so our arrival was probably interpreteted as a manifestation that the gongs were being correctly played, hence the redoubling of their efforts.

The following day I awoke to find that we were sailing westwards in the direction of Bali. The gongs, white rice and catsup had scrambled John's brain to the degree that he was mutinying. I took over the helm and sailed due north in the hope of intercepting better winds and currents, and avoiding coral. As soon as we were far offshore, John started chatting to the spirits again. I then discovered that our compass was behaving as erratically as John. My first reaction was to tell him to pipe down with his mumbo jumbo and explain what he had done to it – such as placing a magnet nearby in a version of Conrad's *End of the Tether*. He protested his innocence, and then I read on the chart that magnetic disturbances were experienced in the vicinity of Tambora volcano, which was our visible landmark onshore.

The strength and direction of the wind tended to improve during the day, but being without a keel we were vulnerable to the strong currents that swirled around close to the coast. The complicated rigging allowed the sail to hinge in all directions, but made it difficult to manage single-handed. In mid-afternoon we entered Dompo Bay, and the wind died again. John, however, had perked up and was even making a few jokes, but I felt it was just a matter of time before his brain started to short-circuit again with unknown consequences. Like us, local craft were tacking backwards and forwards, and every time we came within hailing distance the same thing was shouted: "Ke mana?" "To where?" John and I then tended to shout different things. John optimistically saying Bali, while each time he did that I was provoked into saying a destination further east.

The wind died completely despite the presence of mountains. I always imagined the mountains would never fail to produce something; I suggested John pray properly to the wind spirits, and get us moving again. His response was wailing a dirge to 'Bapak Bali' and to my astonishment the fire smoke on the east shore was blowing one way, while on the west shore it was blowing the other. I crawled into the vomitorium to try and get some sleep.

The approach to Bima is down a narrow channel, a sort of fjord like funnel, and as we got further down the wind strength picked up until a squall was blowing. The *Gin Pahit* skimmed over the waves with a rushing, gurgling sound as the water eddied past the rudder. We were going so fast that I began to wonder how we were going to stop at Bima harbour. John had a maniacal grin on his face which did nothing to reassure me. At the critical moment he swung the boat round and a renting sound cut through the general noise. He had succeeded in the ripping the sail in half.

It was high tide, and the wind produced an uncomfortable chop while we were anchored. I swam ashore to look for a mechanic to service the engine; I found one, and brought him to the wharf, but he disappeared while I was bringing the boat in close. I gave up for the day and went to stay in a lossman, that was as nasty as the Komodo Inn that Mark, Harry and myself had stayed in on our visit. I left John on board to guard our stores and especially the petrol which had been in such short supply when we came before.

It turned out nobody could service the engine so I decided to take it to Surabaya on a local boat carrying red onions. I would be away about a week, so I gave John some money, and hoped for the best. He had located a fellow Balinese, bought some biscuits, had his hair cut, and for the moment was quite placid.

It started to rain for the first time in a long while, and the children celebrated by dancing about in it. Also staying in my lossman was an English anthropologist called Michael Hitchcock who was planning to spend a year in a local village, and a New Zealand couple travelling by yacht. They had taken two months from Auckland and were estimating another two years before reaching England where the wife came from Surrey. In contrast to the surroundings they were immaculately turned out; he even wore a peaked captain's cap when he went ashore looking every inch a commodore. There was, however, reason for this apparent eccentricity; the psychology was to soft-soap Indonesian officialdom which are sensitive to how people dress and will process their paperwork accordingly.

The journey to Surabaya was notable for the thunderstorms that raged; great jagged forks of lightening like distorted laser beams plunged into the sea, seemingly quite close.

On arrival the captain concealed me in a 'secret' cabin, explaining it was so that the local police wouldn't charge him for my presence. Tommy was then unloaded via a back entrance to forestall any more problems and then onto a bicycle-shaw while I followed it in another bicycle-shaw. At the shop where I had originally bought Tommy they reluctantly agreed to service the thing free and replace the parts that were still under 'guarantee'. The boss was on my side but his employees were surly and defensive to the point where a scuffle took place between the boss and an evil-looking mechanic who had been aggressive towards me. I stayed in a well known budget traveller's hostel called the Bamboo Den, where the usual notices were pinned up warning patrons of the latest conmen and women to watch out for in the area and on the local buses and trains. Indonesia must have some of the most ingenious schemers and operators concentrating on petty crime, who with a different outlook and in an environment with more opportunity would do very well. A local student offering 'help' to Mt Bromo was the most notorious at that time.

There is a permanent feeling of powerlessness here; like in any Third World country, to appeal to a higher authority is immediately to create an additional problem, and one is more than likely to become the prisoner rather than the plaintiff. The only way round it is to have a large stock of banknotes that are dispensed like confetti in the wake of one's progress.

Returning to the boat I met the agent who was rubbing his hands together in anticipation as he saw me staggering under Tommy's weight. "That'll be ten thousand for the engine, ten thousand for you, five thousand for a berth, five thousand for your food, five thousand insurance, five thousand tip for the captain and five thousand for me," he said.

"Thank you very much," I replied "It's so nice to feel unexploited," and I paid him as hurriedly as possibly before he could think of any more charges. Behind us crates of books and drinks were being 'run' up the gangplank by youths with sacks draped over their heads like the Ku-Klax-Klan.

Departure was set for the early hours of the morning so I decided to go into town and walk around a bit. Soon an open-faced, friendly individual with two friends started following me around. I tried to ignore them, but eventually as we were passing a police station I thought I would ask the desk officer in charge to tell them I required nothing and to leave me alone. Lack of sleep, food and general frustration had led me to make this unwise move.

The three men of course spun a story that I had asked them to be my guide etc. and they now wanted payment for their services. The policeman naturally reacted like all Third World policeman, "Give me five thousand rupiahs," he said to me. "Of course, of course" I replied and it was put under his hat that was sitting on the desk top. I then got up to go but two solid hands were swiftly placed on either shoulder and I was propelled back into the sitting position.

"Show me your watch," said the policeman. He was unimpressed. "How much money have you got?" Things were getting out of hand. I was carrying all my money on me as being less of a risk than leaving it on the boat. “It’s in my lossman,” I said. “I’ll go and fetch the fee for these gentlemen, and come back. “One of my men will come with you,” said the policeman, and a thuggish-looking creature escorted me to a becak. Meanwhile the policeman was dividing up the money I had given him.

The joys of travel were once more upon me. As a sense of desperation welled up inside me I decided to leap out at a set of traffic lights and run like a stag. I arrived back at the quay feeling reasonably well disposed towards the people there, but an unpleasant Maduranese, with dark, smooth skin, tousled hair and an evil smile accosted me and started warning me against gangsters which made me suspect he knew more than he was letting on.

The throng of humanity around the docks was more active in the middle of the night than by day because it was cooler. A noisy game of badminton was being played by some transvestites. The air smelt of cloves, and cheap scent. I found my boat, which had now been loaded with hundreds of chairs - for some inexplicable reason, because nobody I had seen in the Nusa Tenggara islands used them.

At dawn the engine started with a roar and we eased out in to the Madura Strait. We followed the Java coast all day, which was mostly covered in low cloud. The many volcanoes occasionally peered through the cloud bank. Bali appeared in the late afternoon. It doesn’t look hospitable from a distance, Mt Agung dominating a patchwork of browns, greens and greys. The first Dutch ship to go there was very surprised to find the island and its inhabitants totally different from its neighbours by having a friendly Hindu population, and it took two years for all the crew to be rounded up and the ship to set sail again. The ship’s menu was the usual diet of rice with a little something like fish soup at 8.00 in the morning and 5.00 in the afternoon. Before eating, a few old hadjis on board went through their washing routine with such grim seriousness that it almost became comedy.

The sea round about was littered with the hideous debris of industrial society, and the attractive debris of biodegradable hindu offerings that had floated out from Bali. The crew explained that the two lots of debris were linked - a boat had sunk. The sea is unpredictable in this area of deep troughs and strong currents, and for two hours we had rough seas despite moderate winds. Things calmed again, but during the night passing Lombok and the Alas Strait there was more chop with the spray lashing up to the top of the cabin.

At five in the morning we found a swamped sampan. Like pirates, the younger members of the crew swarmed onto it, untying the sarong that had been tied onto one of the rattan mast stays. They eagerly ripped open the pack of cigarettes they found, discarded with disgust the damp ones, and distributed the others; similarly with the small amount of money. One of them put on the sarong and paraded around in it. Although it was obvious what had happened I asked where the owner was. "Orang mati" "He's dead," was the gleeful reply as they cut away the mast and rigging prior to an unsuccessful attempt to float it. "Where do you think he's from?" I asked. "Maddang island," they answered; and that became the end of the matter, the only reminder being the red patterned sarong proudly worn by its new owner.

I cooked up an alternative theory to the sampan mystery: the sarong was of a type worn by tourists in Bali, and not local fishermen, the cigarettes were an expensive imported brand, and I had personally heard the first reaction of our crew saying to each other they thought it was a Westerner. A short while later a motor launch had approached us with a European on board; above the noise and our uncooperative crew they were gesticulating in the direction of the sunk sampan and trying to ask questions. Eventually they had given up and gone off in the direction of Moyo and Satonda islands where some Europeans were working on a timber project.

The outlines of this area were beginning to become familiar, like people whom one sees but doesn't know. The massive volcano of Rinjani, the islands of Moyo, Satonda, Maddang, and Dompo Bay. Only the colours changed. The long strip from Satonda island to Dompo Bay was now different shades of green, more like a rain forest, with the permanent browns nearer the coast, and an emerald green haze of paddy shoots against the scorched earth, black from burning off. Heavy white clouds with pale grey linings turning the usually blue sea a dull dun.

The many dolphins following the boat never seemed to take the fishing line baits for some reason. There was no wind, and as we passed a becalmed sailing boat I thought of the *Gin Pahit* in the same position ten days ago.

As we came within a day of reaching Bima, I began to feel excitement at the prospect of getting back to the *Gin Pahit*; it suddenly seemed like home, and would, extraordinary as it may seem, be more comfortable than this boat after the past few days. The apprehension and anticipation at the thought of John's latest antics was almost enough to conquer my constipation, something the filthiest of food, handled with the filthiest of hands, had failed to do on the boat. (In general throughout the area, the poor diet tended to torment ones intestines with alternate bouts of dysentery and constipation.)

The captain was a young Christian from Manado, very pleasant but as such arousing the enmity of the surly Moslem crew who referred to him as 'puteh' - 'white' - presumably because they saw him as an Uncle Tom type character, or perhaps because of his similarity to the superior light-skinned jungle folk.

Once again the wind picked up strength in the Bima channel, and we arrived in the late afternoon. The *Gin Pahit* was there, John was there, anchored next to two other Balinese boats. A mountain of empty cigarette packets littered the floor, the *warung* was coated in grime and grease, the torch and lamp were broken, and the sail very unsatisfactorily 'repaired'. However, I had a spare sail stored in the bottom of the boat and the mere presence of both John and the boat was as much as I had dared hope for and I was content.

# Chapter 10

## *John-Robin Goes Mad*

As I say, the nature of Indonesian food seems to produce alternate bouts of constipation and gut-clutching dysentery, but unfortunately it's impossible to predict in advance what's coming next. My days on the MV Halia Harapan eating food flavoured with cockroaches and rat droppings had sealed me up like cement, but it took the scrapings of a bean dish in the lossman Lila Braha to activate a healthy bout of the shits. No doubt the fact that the lossman was short of water had put a curb on its already rudimentary hygene. I also had the alarming experience of seeing my faeces jump out of the lavatory pan after I'd crapped on top of a toad that had settled in there.

In the same way that a heavy fall of snow in the UK produces the sort of chaos that suggests it has never snowed there before, the heavy rainfall in tropical Third World countries somehow cannot be harnessed and fed through the pipes. There might be a torrent falling from the sky, but the pipes in the plumbing system offer a thin trickle. Even a country like Brunei, with all its available financial resources, regularly has the water cut off during the day.

The emaciated ponies, permanently harnessed in their carts, chewed lackadaisically on the foul-looking forage, bloody raw patches shining over rump bones where their masters repeatedly struck them with their goads. Their condition reminded me of the pictures of donkeys and ex-cavalry horses from the First World War that had been left behind in Egypt to be used and abused by the local trades people. In fact it's a familiar sight throughout the Middle East. In Libya I recall that every donkey had deep raw patches around their ankles where the hobble ropes had cut into them, it's one of the chasms between that world and the western world.

I picked up my baggage from the police, bought some supplies, and set off at 3 o'clock in the afternoon. John had gone into one of his moods again, compounded by a bad back from lying around so long so that he couldn't help with anything heavy. He'd reverted to the awkward attitude he had when we left Bali. He now said he was going no further than Maumere. A new ploy was to contradict all the good things that he and Made Monoh had originally said about the boat when they wanted to sell it; now suddenly the bamboo outriggers were old and leaked, the sail was of poor quality and liable to tear again - that was obvious, as it had been so badly repaired by John himself, and anyway that was why I had brought a spare one in the bottom of the boat.

In the early hours of the morning we came close to Sangeang island, and at one point for half an hour hit very turbulent water caused undoubtedly by undersea earthquakes and volcanic activity which are happening all the time. Sangeang island is an active volcano rising to over 6,000 feet, and smoke and hot rock were belching from the sides. MV City King reported in 1964 seeing red hot streams of lava flowing down from a distance of twenty two miles. The pilot book refers to the island as being reef-fringed with great depth offshore, but when we had come this way before we had unexpectedly hit a very shallow patch.

At dawn the east star produced Komodo about five miles south. I streamed the new fishing gear, and tied it round my leg in a slip-knot in the local style, so one immediately knows when one has hooked something. Within moments a large shark clamped itself onto the line and nearly pulled me out of the boat. The knot had failed to come apart. John came to my assistance, but was unable to hold it either. The shark, six feet long, thrashed out of the water and in doing so bit through the line.

John took the incident as an omen, and embarked on a series of black magic stories that all had their point in suggesting we go back or that he had suddenly lost his physical strength.

"Wetar island it is, John," I repeated automatically to his gloomy words. "We'll anchor off Gili Bodo island and have a rest. The translation of the name of this island is 'Mad Stupid island', and it proved to be a genuine omen.

After diving for some cowrie shells, I returned to the boat to prepare some food, and after burrowing around to get a tin of sardines, turned round to find John standing threateningly with a knife. "Yes, John?" I asked as though he was offering to peel some potatoes.

"Fighting," he replied.

"Don't be a fool and put it away. If you want to go back, then go from Maumere, I can find somebody else there, and you will also be able to get a boat from there."

"No, I want to go from Reo, it must be Reo," he insisted.

Reo was the furthest point east that we had gone with Made, and maybe his behaviour was caused by his apprehension of 'unknown' territory. He had regularly referred to the dreaded 'Orang Timor' - 'Eastern Men' and now he probably felt he was actually going to come face to face with them.

"Alright, we'll go into Reo," I said.

Instead of being cheerful, John decided to call up his Hindu gods for whatever purpose, and endless incantations started. My patience was further strained when he prevented me from using the useful thermos mug for keeping drinks hot, because it had been incorporated into one of his mumbo-jumbo rites.

Dawn found us off Reo bay. The sight made John quite playful; he started performing the Hindu muscle exercises similar to types of Chinese exercises that Westerners perform on Bali's beaches, grinning and repeating, "I'm going back".

The tide was out and the river was too low to get up so we anchored in shallow water over a mud-flat. I gave him his money, which he most certainly hadn't earned, and five minutes to get off the boat.

After all this performance he refused to get out and walk, the boat couldn't go any closer, so I was faced with brute force. I would like to be able to say that a left upper cut sent his hat spinning into the sea like a flying saucer, he went after it, and was last seen heading for the shore in an untidy doggie paddle. Instead he and his bag were bundled over the side.

This was enough to trigger him running amok, a condition local to that part of the world, that has entered the English language. He scrambled back on board, grabbed a paddle and started waving it around like a Japanese martial arts fighter. After I had relieved him of that he produced a knife, and made some half hearted lunges at me. Suddenly he came to his senses, and burst into great loud sobs of tears saying "Bapak Bali oooh, Bapak Bali oooh."

This noise alerted some hominoids who appeared from behind a nearby mud-bank and started mimicking him. The whole incident was making me feel sick through conflicting emotions. The boat needed two people to sail it, but I didn't need John's mad behaviour; however, it was so childlike that I felt guilty of bullying him. Yet there was no time to ponder on this metaphysical problem because the tide was still running out, and the boat was threatening to get stranded. I had to start moving it, at which point John finally decided to go.

As he set off he turned and apologised for everything, I don't know whether the Hindu religion overlaps Christianity on matters of forgiveness, but I muttered something that hopefully could have been interpreted any way he chose, and turned my attention forwards, to the matter in hand.

# Chapter 11

## *Ewang the Bugis Signs On*

I got the engine started, and almost immediately got tangled up in some fishing nets. After untangling myself from them, I sped away. It was early evening by this time, and I had already been on watch since the previous midnight. I was totally exhausted but needed to go a bit further to find a safe anchorage. First I had to get more fuel into the tank, but while concentrating on this I drifted onto a coral bank, and in extricating myself from it cut my legs on the coral. I was also handicapped by not having practiced the two most important knots - one securing the rudder in a configuration that enabled it to snap a piece of wood and break free rather than being damaged itself when hitting something, and the other holding the complicated mast and sail arrangement together. I soon had rope burns.

I was also worried about falling overboard. I anchored in coral off Toro Padang, and sank into an exhausted sleep. Although the coast always looks deserted, little boats invariably emerge from some small recess. Prior to the Industrial Revolution in England, when the population was more evenly spread, no doubt straw chewing yokels emerged from every copse in a similar way.

It meant that in addition to the physical complications of carrying out two-man jobs single handed, being alone made me vulnerable, and a target for pirates.

With two or more people, each is dependent on the other. Every action or decision, one explains to oneself, is either for oneself or for the other person or both, and because it's impossible to wholly apportion which, this leads to self-deception. I remember Tony Benn saying it was much easier to be unscrupulous for a cause than for oneself, which apart from being an interesting comment in the light of his own career, is on the same lines. "I did this for you, to help you, or I was trying my best for both of us," is a piece of self-delusion that is almost impossible to unravel.

Alone everything is for oneself, every action directly affects one person only; under these conditions self-deception is impossible, and possibly it leads to insight and integrity in dealing with other people.

I left at 5 o'clock the following morning after I had seen a Bugis boat hovering around. We sailed along in tandem, but not communicating. I copied what he did with his sails to try and learn something, but I was less sure of the situation when I carried out some experiment, and saw him doing the same thing. It was a case of those car stickers that read 'Don't follow me I'm lost'.

With nobody to talk to, the boat became semi-personalised; and like a bicycle in its sensitivity, I could feel the smallest thing that affected its overall balance, such as a change in current or tide.

I reached Tanjong Karterbileh in the evening and anchored for the night. In the morning I was about to do some diving when a knot of glowering hominoids appeared from a recess and tried to board. I fobbed them off and motored away, leaving the Bugis boat that had anchored on the other side of the island.

Like most days it was incredibly hot, but I had nobody to share the watches, so I began to fry and doze. It was necessary to cover up, so sweat rashes appeared, and the handling of the sail became very tiring because it had no pulleys to reduce the tension. Rolling it up also became a problem because the boat needed to be kept head to wind during the process otherwise the strength of the wind just unrolled it again; as it was done at the front of the boat, the position of the vomitorium made it impossible to rig up an extension from there to the tiller.

By the evening, I felt as though I had been driving down the M1, non-stop, for a week; my head was lolling around, my eyes glazed, but I still needed to get to a safe anchorage.

Suddenly the rudder stick went off like a pistol shot, my head snapped awake, and in a reflex action I lifted Tommy out of the water in the nick of time. This was immediately followed by the sound of graunching coral as the boat ploughed into a reef. This is where the sturdy, single log, design is indispensable. Nothing of major damage had taken place. However, I'm sure that a type of centreboard could be set up along the same lines as the rudder, which would make a big difference to the lateral drift; but they don't do it, and there must be a good reason for it.

Having fully woken up I made out pencils of light dotted around, and realised that they were fishing boats fishing around the reef. My first instinct was relief that help was at hand, but this was Indonesia, and it was rapidly followed by the realisation that they might regard me as a large stranded fish.

Some of them paddled over, and after peering through the gloom, started a mocking ribald laughter. They made no sign of wanting to help, which was probably just as well.

The tide was running out, and as soon as it was low enough I carried the anchor to the deepest spot so that I could pull myself off as soon as the tide turned. I then tried to get some sleep, but soon the inevitable happened - I became aware of some unnatural movement on the boat, opened the flaps of the vomitorium and found a couple of friendly Indonesians about to help themselves to the engine. This was an occasion when I needed to take a tip from Captain Slocum who put tin tacks on the deck of his boat so that the resulting howl of an intruder would wake him up.

A.R. Wallace describes an experience with coral which I had no trouble recognising:

About ten o'clock we ran full onto a coral reef, which alarmed us a good deal, but luckily got safe off again. About two in the afternoon we reached an extensive coral reef, and were sailing close alongside it, when the wind suddenly dropped and we drifted on to it before we could get in our heavy main sail, which we were obliged to let run down and fall partly overboard. We had much difficulty in getting off, but at last got into deep water again though with reefs and islands all around us. At night we did not know what to do, as no one on board could tell us where we were or what dangers might surround us, the only one of our crew who was acquainted with the coast having been left on the island. We therefore took in all sail and allowed ourselves to drift, as we were some miles from the nearest land. A light breeze, however, sprang up, and about midnight we found ourselves again bumping over a coral reef. As it was very dark, and we knew nothing of our position, we could only guess how to get off again, and had there been a little more wind we might have been knocked to pieces. However, in about half an hour we did get off, and then thought it best to anchor on the edge of the reef until morning.

The admiralty pilot for the whole of this area qualified all its information with "Anchorage may be obtained by vessels with local knowledge." This is hardly surprising when coral can grow at the rate of an inch a year soon rendering depths on charts out of date.

All these charts were made by the British Admiralty, and it must have been quite a job compiling them. Many of the descriptions of people and places are entertaining as well as useful. I met somebody whose father worked on them at the end of the last century. Months and years were spent gathering information which was followed by months at home writing them up. It must have been a fascinating job.

During the night the tide turned, and I was able to pull myself off, and gingerly set off, but like the Charge of the Light Brigade, there was coral to the front, left and right. By dawn I had conned my way to just offshore a village, not far by my calculation from Maumere. I chucked the anchor into the sandy bottom, and hailed a fisherman in a sampan.

Fortunately he was friendly, and suggested I anchor just off his hut perched on stilts at the water's edge.

The sail by this time had about thirty holes in it and was very thin. John's repairs had been about as useless as I would have expected, but no matter, I had a spare sail, along with all the jerrycans of valuable fuel stored in the bottom of the boat. I moved everything to get at it, and made an interesting discovery: dear John had sold the sail and three quarters of the fuel. No doubt the Balinese in Bima had persuaded him, if he had needed persuading. Nevertheless, at the time, I had an open mind, thinking it could have been stolen when he wasn't around. I found it hard to believe that even he would have jeopardised not only my safety but my ability to keep going by committing such a dastardly deed. But events proved otherwise; he later admitted it with some feeble excuse about thinking we wouldn't have needed it if we had gone straight back from Bima. But such was John's half-baked character that I couldn't get as angry with him as he deserved.

At this hopeless juncture, fate took a hand. The fisherman proved not only to be an organiser, but volunteered to be a crewman. His wife was heavily pregnant, and he was keen to earn some money for the anticipated extra expenditure of having another child.

The village was called Kampong Wuring, and I shall remember it with gratitude. (Sadly this is one of several villages in the area that disappeared under a tidal wave in 1992, following an earthquake offshore, killing all inhabitants.)

While I nursed the sores and rashes that had developed from the coral off Reo, a swarm of villagers descended on the boat, removed the sail, brought some new sailcloth, cut out a new sail, and stitched it all the way round by hand. All they wanted for this was an endless supply of Commodore cigarettes.

While this was being done I disappeared into a mangrove swamp to select a new piece of wood to replace the rudder safety stick. Inside the swamp was a terrible unswattable fly, that refused to die after it had been forcefully thwacked.

The fisherman was called Ewang and was a buginese from Macassar. He was a traditional sea-rover with a taste for piracy, and an outsider in the village. This combined with his wife's confinement made his coming with me easier. He scrubbed the hull of the boat with coconut husks, coiled up the ropes properly and addressed me as 'Chief', instead of the dreaded 'Mister' (which is used for European women as well).

I went into Maumere to get some supplies. There was no sign of the transvestites at the Lossman Bogor, instead a lounging Chinaman from Solo who insisted on playing chess for money. I played to lose quickly in order to get moving, but I won, and left, and probably forestalled his plan to double the stakes and nail me on the next game.

The police station was next to the bemo stand which was awkward. In Indonesia it's no good thinking you can avoid 'trouble' just by looking inoffensive, because the police are on the lookout for just that type of newcomer to whom they can ask a few friendly questions and 'discover by chance' that you are not quite in order to the point of requiring a little baksheesh to turn a blind eye.

They would certainly have been informed of what was going on at the village, and when I saw them looking at me as I set off with my supplies, I knew, that they knew, that I knew, they would be along fairly promptly to collect their cigarette money, or in the case of a 'boat owner' something more substantial, before I set off into the wild blue yonder.

So when I got back to the boat. I hurried up Ewang, who was saying his prayers, while his wife hovered around tearfully asking me to look after him.

Many hands make light work creating a new sail

# Chapter 12

## *From Temple to Mosque*

I produced the chart for Wetar. I didn't want any confusion this time on where we were going, and asked him with his 'local knowledge' for a suitable anchorage to head for. He studied the diagram with a glazed uncomprehending expression, and then slowly pointed at a bay. I squinted at the small type, 'Labuan Ayer Panas', - 'Hot Water Harbour'. This was where I had originally aimed to get to, and I was glad we were thinking along the same lines.

"That's okay, Chief," he said, with the mechanical smile that Asians consider such an important part of their culture.

"Oh, one more thing before we leave, I want 1000 rupiahs a day, not the 500 rupiahs that we agreed."

"Yes, that's fine," I answered, feeling cautiously satisfied, in that he had behaved in a predictable way, achieved what he wanted, and we were both agreed on the correct rate. "Now let's go," and I started the engine while his wife was trying to prompt him into asking for something else. He scrambled aboard and we picked our way round the sand bars, coral shoals and submerged rocks. I marvelled at how I had got in at night without mishap. Some dolphins or 'Lumba Lumba' as they are locally called escorted us out to open sea, and I felt incredibly relieved to be under way. Unknown at the time was the fact that the police had duly arrived while we were still in sight. When I heard about it later I tried to feel the corresponding relief against the inevitable hassle and expense that had been so narrowly avoided. We enjoy positive good fortune, curse at bad luck, and prefer not to think about 'what might have happened' indeed it's considered 'boring' by many people to discuss this side of life, but like our memory, it strikes me as an under-utilised conversational topic.

I don't know the attitude of other cultures to memories, whether it's treated with the same suspicion as in the West "Look forwards my son, not backwards" - or regarded as a sensation to be developed and made pleasurable, but to me the joy of a past memory equals the anticipation of something new.

The new sail fitted better than I expected, it didn't roll up completely but it was a huge improvement on what was there before. Petrol was now severely rationed, which meant long periods becalmed and overheating. There were days when I felt as though we and the boat might spontaneously combust such was the limpid, unrelieved heat. The sea became, as in Kipling's 'Mary Gloster', 'Oily, and treacly'.

As Ewang was a Moslem the boat now became a mosque instead of John's temple. At the spot where the smell and curling smoke of joss sticks, accompanied by high-pitched mumbo-jumbo, had arisen there was now a prayer mat on which Ewang crouched four times a day while producing a nasal, whining incantation. The two religions had converged on their choice of site to worship, a factor that has produced many a problem in the wider world.

The wind behaved erratically throughout the night, and by dawn it had died completely. Usually the early morning and evening brought some breeze as the land heated up or cooled off.

We were off Pulau Babi, 'Pig Island', and we anchored on the coral reef, which dropped away almost vertically. Some inquisitive locals came to observe us, and then drifted away again. Like in most of this area underwater turbulence caused a choppy sea despite very little wind. In the 1992 earthquake this island disappeared completely. Perhaps the fault line ran down the vertical reef edge.

Ewang wearing the hat

A ntle breeze picked up, and we were able to get as far as Tanjong Bunga, about the most northern point on Flores, and close to its eastern end. Ewang was respectful, unassuming and hard-working. He hadn't however, had much, if any, experience of this type of craft, and looked to me for direction and knowledge. It was the blind leading the blind. We ended up rerigging the sail according to our own specifications, and hoping for the best.

During the long nights slowly sailing or virtually becalmed I had plenty of time to observe the 'celestial bodies', the moon and stars moving across the sky during the night, just as the sun does during the day, the moon rising and setting later, and of course changing shape. If I had had a reference book with me, I could have filled in those long hours learning to identify the night sky. As it is, my knowledge of the cosmos is pre-Copernican and I'm hard pressed to spot the North Star or Southern Cross.

Unmistakable however, was the bright star that appeared at dusk, and another one at dawn, although I'm told it's actually one and the same, namely Venus. As usual, after the event, I bought a guide to the stars, but am still waiting for a suitable opportunity to try and work things out.

Our next destination was Adonara island, also known as the 'Isle of Murderers' in recognition of battles between the hill folk and the coastal dwellers. Feuds lasting hundreds of years regularly culminate in battles that make the troubles in Northern Ireland seem tame by comparison. Portuguese missionaries have introduced Catholic practices to the islands, which, like Northern Ireland, may or may not have contributed to intolerance, but they run hand in hand with spear-brandishing, war-painted citizens with hate and righteousness in equal measures on their minds.

Close to Adonara are Solor and Alor islands. The Portuguese had been a vigorous presence in the islands from at least the early sixteenth century; they built forts, proselytised, traded and inter-married. Sandalwood was the most popular item of trade, and became the islands' 'Tree of Destiny'. Over exploited, it hardly exists now. In Western Australia I met the heirs of these early sandalwood-traders, loners ranging over the outback collecting the straggly dead-looking branches lying at the base of small trees. I also met other similar types tracking down rogue dingoes, and culling kangaroos. Long may there survive areas of the world for these people to live before it's 'made verminous by humanity'.

Lacking 'local knowledge' I turned to the pilot book. It's compiler had obviously faced some of the same problems. It referred to smoke and sulphur continually rising from one of the volcanoes, but that 'the local inhabitants have no knowledge of any eruption having taken place'. But it continued by saying, 'It should be remembered that this area is subject to intense volcanic activity, and the possibility of underwater eruptions leading to great depth changes cannot be excluded.'

The Alor Strait between Lomblen and Pantar obviously contained further complications and the survey vessel decided not to hang around longer than necessary. The following description gave me something to think about:

*A vessel with no reserve of power should not attempt to pass through the Alor Strait from the North during the South East monsoon, as, with the predominating south winds, it is impractical to get through on one tide. The horizontal movement of the water in the Alor Strait is of a semi-diurnal character, and may attain a considerable rate. Owing to the lack of anchorage in the Strait it was impossible to carry out any thorough observations during the survey. The following general information, obtained from the local inhabitants and checked by observations, gives a fairly good idea of the prevailing tidal streams. The tidal streams mainly follow the direction of the strait, throughout. During the South East Monsoon the SW-going stream lasts longer and is stronger than the NE-going stream. It has been observed that the SW-going stream flowed from about two hours to about nine hours after the moon's passage, and the NE-going stream for the remaining hours. During the North West Monsoon the NE-going stream is presumably of longer duration and stronger than the SW-going stream.*

*Spring tidal streams appear to occur two to three days after the full moon and the new moon, and neaps from two to three days after the quarters. The rate at springs averages five to six knots. The maximum rate can probably be expected when the spring tides occur during the period of the moon's greatest declination either south or north, and particularly the years that the moon's declination is greater than the sun's declination.*

*Off projecting points and around the islands the direction and rate of the tidal streams are naturally irregular. In the North part of the Strait the rate of the tidal streams is considerably less than in the South part, except close off Tanjung Leur where a rate of five knots was observed.*

My reaction to this type of description was that anything could happen at any time. I did try to follow up the question of the moon's passage by writing to the Hydrographer of the Navy and got this reply from Commander N.C. Glen, MNI,RN, Superintendent Tidal Branch:

*The expression "moon's passage" is becoming obsolete and where the data is available is replaced by the reference to the time of HW at a convenient port. It should be extended to read 'the time of the moon's passage over the meridian of the place'.*

*The Nautical Almanac contains daily values of the time, in GMT., of the moon's Upper and Lower passages over the meridian of Greenwich. The Upper passage is when the moon is on this side of the earth and the Lower when it is on the other side.*

*This can also be taken to be the Zone Time of the moon's passage over the meridian of the Time Zone provided a correction for longitude is applied. A table giving these corrections is included at the back of the Nautical Almanac.*

*The calculation of tidal events, HW,LW, etc., by reference to the time of the moon's meridian passage was a common procedure before the introduction of more comprehensive tide tables.*

This still left me a bit confused, but I hope it may help somebody else reading it.

Poised to cross the Alor Strait, the pilot book's information hadn't immediately suggested the best time to set off. Ewang said, "You decide, Chief", when I had suggested his nautical instincts might be more useful than the book's information.

"Well, now is as good a time as any" was my response to that, and away we went. It proved to be a very fast sail. All the elements referred to were happening at once. A steep sea and strong wind were flowing up from the south, and as we were going east, we were surfing along the waves, and just flipping over the top of them before they broke. Ewang was on the helm and enjoying himself: "Lihat, Chief, dia lari" "Look, Chief, she's flying along." I was inside the vomitorium praying that the bamboo floats would hold up to the increased strain.

My chart showed a large drying reef directly in our path. I warned him about it, but, like John, he didn't believe that a chart or pilot book could somehow magically predict what was around. In the event, he just spotted the reef in time, and we turned sharp north, made our way round it, and arrived at the northern tip of Pantar island.

I opened up the doors at the front of the vomitorium, and was struck by a different profile; something was missing. I then realised that the anchor, and the long coil of rope to which it was attached had slipped over the side as we surfed at alarming angles along the sides of the waves. I don't know what would have happened if the other end of the rope had been attached to the boat. Instead, into my mind came the words of the song 'Three wheels on my wagon'.

Not surprisingly A.R. Wallace had also had trouble with his anchor:

*Now, however, came the climax of our troubles. The swell produced by the squall made us jerk our cable a good deal, and it suddenly snapped low down in the water. We drifted out to sea, and immediately set our main sail, but we were now without any anchor, and in a vessel so poorly manned that it could not be rowed against the most feeble current or the slightest wind, it would be madness to approach these dangerous shores except in the most perfect calm. We had also only three days' food left. It was therefore out of the question making any further attempts to get round the point without assistance, and I at once determined to run to the village of Gani-Diluer, about ten miles further north, where we understood there was a good harbour, and where we might get provisions and a few more rowers. Hitherto winds and currents had invariably opposed our passage southwards and we might have expected them to be favourable to us now we had turned our bowsprit in an opposite direction. But it immediately fell calm, and then after a time a westerly land breeze set in, which would not serve us, and we had to row again for hours, and when night came had not reached the village. We were so fortunate however as to find a deep sheltered cove where the water was quite smooth, and we constructed a temporary anchor by filling a sack with stones from our ballast, which being well secured by a network of rattans held us safely during the night. The next morning my men went on shore to cut wood suitable for making fresh anchors, and at about noon, the current turning in our favour, we proceeded to the village where we found an excellent and well protected anchorage.*

# Chapter 13

## Hot Water Harbour

After the strong blow across the Alor Strait we were becalmed in uncomfortable chop off the north of Pantar island. The sea was bubbling and boiling in different places, no doubt from the seabed volcanic activity. That and the active volcanoes along the coast were presumably the reason for our compass behaving erratically. We spent the night bobbing off Tanjong Matari.

The next morning produced the sort of oppressive heat that can only be relieved by a thunderstorm, which duly obliged. It was accompanied by wind, but we were both so tired that we wasted it, and had to sleep. Our food was now white rice, chilli sauce and biscuits. I had relied on being able to get some supplies along the coast, but this had proved impossible. The pilot had mentioned one place as providing 'limited provisions such as chickens, pigs and goats', but when we got there the village had moved on, or been washed away in the last tidal wave.

Alor island was more wooded than the other islands, and very mountainous. It was cultivated near the coast, and burnt in places, but overall it looked more appealing. However, we didn't stop. Wetar was close, and I wanted to push on.

My life had come to revolve entirely around the state of the wind; if it was blowing we had to keep moving, when it died we slept, but this was often impossible as the heat during the day was suffocating.

We drifted on an oil-and-treacle sea towards Kamping island, just north of Timor and part of the former Portuguese colony of East Timor. The sound of gunfire could be heard from the Indonesian army suppressing resistance to their invasion. The Indonesian invasion of East Timor in the 1970s has been consistently resisted by the local population whose 400 years under Catholic Portugal means they have little in common with the Indonesians. At the time of the invasion they were thought to have been a potential Communist threat, and most Western countries turned a blind eye, although none of them, bar Australia, has accepted the legality of the invasion. Australia was keen to carve up the oil exploration area in the Timor Sea, and therefore came to an understanding with Indonesia, despite the fact that several Australian journalists were shot dead covering the original invasion. More lately a protest march in Dili resulted in a large number of local people being shot dead. Widespread demonstrations in Australia took place, but government policy hasn't changed. The best hope for the East Timorese is the work being done by Portugal within the United Nations.

We came close to the shore of Kamping island, and like many of the other islands there was a fringe of trees and vegetation along a narrow coastal strip, against a back drop of denuded, dried up hills. Vegetation sprang out from the cracks and gullies which ferried the rain-water off the hillsides. Forests can never return here as the humus and topsoil with its fragile sponge-like action has long been washed away leaving barren rock to carry the rain-water away in flash floods. On the flat coastal strip enough soil has remained to promote coconut trees and other plants necessary for day to day life but lacking the island's former glorious diversity and attractiveness. Finally, of course, the removal of cover has made it much hotter.

We limped up the coast of Kambing in a north easterly direction heading for Liran island. Ewang's cooperative, calm manner, in contrast to the antics of John-Robin, had put my blood pressure somewhere back to normal.

At the south of Liran island was the wreck of a lighthouse, formerly erected by the Dutch. Routes through the islands are sometimes used by large vessels going to Australia.

Gradually Wetar Island shimmered out of the horizon. A.R. Wallace had described it as follows:

*Turning off towards Banda we passed Pulau Kambing, Wetar and Roma, all of which are desolate and barren volcanic islands, almost as uninviting as Aden, and offering a strange contrast to the usual verdure and luxuriance of the archipelago.*

The pilot book stated:

*The coasts of Pulau Wetar are high, steep and inhospitable and there are practically no anchorages. The island is very sparsely inhabited in the interior, and the inhabitants live in villages along the coasts, but here the climate is unhealthy.*

It was this description that had first attracted me to the island as a suitable location for Asian refugees. It may not have been better, but it was more appropriate than old barracks in a disused airfield in the south of England, from which they would rapidly graduate via council housing to affluence while at the same time providing outdoor relief for busybody social workers.

My first impression of Wetar was a mixture of both the above descriptions. From a distance it was impressive: mountainous and thickly forested. Clearly its difficult access had saved it from the attention of wood-cutters, and prevented its population from growing too large. Apart from a Western-style tanker on the horizon, I had seen no local craft for two days. Even Ewang had no ready explanation for its desolate appearance. The pilot book had referred to the unhealthy coastline - perhaps there had been a great plague, news of which we would have to bear to the outside world.

We sailed between the north of Liran island and Nautilus reef, on guard for the whirlpools and heavy chop marked on the chart. The small size of the boat meant we could have disappeared into one of the whirlpools, and then been spat out in pieces from the fissured, coral-covered seabed. There was an abundance of fish all the way across the reef.

It was dark as we approached the corner of Hot Water Harbour. Over the mountainside there were pinpricks of light from fires, demonstrating that there were indeed some inhabitants. We tried to find our way into the bay, but nearly hit some rocks and decided to go out a little and wait until the morning.

During the night the wind, encouraged by the mountains picked up, and blew us back to our starting point. Although I had been asleep when this happened, I accepted it had been unintentional and not similar to John's tactics of getting a message over. Asian politeness requires that instead of saying something unpalatable to the recipient of bad news, you waste his time instead and hope that a compromise can be arrived at. The logical and actual conclusion to this method, if neither party wants to give way, is amok. The individual suddenly snaps and lashes out murderously at anybody within range, and can only be stopped by drastic measures. John had already gone over the top, and I didn't want another case with Ewang; no doubt he was dreaming of his wife and new-born, and felt he had gone far enough. The idea of resettling Vietnamese refugees on this island was as crazy to him as it was to Mr Chips the fishmonger in Burley-New-Town, England having them as his neighbour.

The other reason that amok has become an accepted method of expression is because the wide diversity of languages throughout the archipelago has reduced the availability of words to talk out a problem; this leaves people to pick up the signals of growing disatisfaction, and act accordingly or expect an amok on their hands.

Calmly, and watching carefully for any signs of approaching madness, I told Ewang we were going back to Wetar, and landing at Hot Water Harbour. He was too tired to do anything other than nod resignedly, and go off to sleep while I coaxed the Gin Pahit back towards Diroro Tutun. The island was studded with 'Tutun's' my dictionary didn't have the word, but I assume it meant 'point'. All of them were attached to Indonesian names, except for a rocky promontory in the south called Eden Tutun, which I imagine was named in a fanciful moment by a sailor from a cooler climate.

By midday we were back in the bay. It was a beautful location. A wide gently sloping sandy beach surrounded the bay. A few grass shelters were dotted along the shore, with coconut trees and long grass. The pilot book mentioned a village at the head of the inlet, but there was no sign of it from offshore. The sun was at its zenith, and the oily, treacly sea was melting both us and the boat. I stuck a stick in the sand and tied the boat to that. We still had no anchor, and it was a priority to sort something out.

Hot Water Harbour, Wetar Island

At the back of the beach it was swampy, with no apparent access inland. Huge shade trees provided relief from the sun. We pushed through the jungle and either a crocodile or Komodo dragon squirmed out of our path into a swamp pool. I felt nervous with nobody about. A cockerel crowed. "See," said Ewang, "there is a village."

"Okay you find it," I said.

He soon returned to say he had seen the chickens running towards the hills but no sign of a village. I then went to have a look, and discovered that his chickens were jungle fowl, which happen to crow like domestic chickens.

We both agreed that this place was a non-starter and to make our way along the coast until we reached a village. First, however, we had some boiled rice and a rest; then a swim in the bay, the only time I swam for pleasure on the whole trip. I cooked the rice in sea water on the basis of it being ready-salted, and found it tasted okay. Ewang wasn't too sure.

Later we tacked out of the bay, and hadn't gone very far before reaching a coastal village at the head of a wide area of coral. An armada of sampans came off, and tried to board. Ewang was trying to make them understand that we had no anchor, and could they bring one. In their inquisitiveness nobody wanted to be bothered to arrange this. I saw a Bugis boat just leaving, and swung the *Gin Pahit* round to go after them and see if they had a spare one. The crowded scene, and bucking surf, guaranteed an accident, but fortunately it was a minor one; one of the villagers was standing in the water, wearing a pair of sunglasses that he had put on for the occasion, and was intending to escort me ashore.

However, the bamboo outrigger caught him under an arm, and catapulted him arse over tip.

Ewang could of course converse with the Bugis boat, but they took one look at the engine and assessed that we could afford to pay the extortionate sum of 100,000 rupiahs. We declined the offer, and left them to carry on to Dili, the capital of East Timor, a short distance to the south.

We then spotted some enterprising natives jumping up and down on the shore trying to attract our attention to a large angulated block of coral through which there was a hole. It was a makeshift anchor, and after attaching a rope through the hole, it served its purpose well. A locally used item for local conditions always works, however unlikely it may seem to an outsider's eyes. The angulated coral wedged itself in the coral reef, and later was equally effective in a rocky seabed. It cost nothing, providing an example that the best things in life are sometimes free.

I was now ready to be escorted to the presence of the chief. He turned out to be a very civilised man sitting quietly wearing glasses (I hoped it wasn't him to whom I had given a ducking), poised with a fountain pen and piece of paper to take down my details. He knew Australia, but he hadn't heard of England - the first person in authority, in my travels, to have claimed that distinction.

Later he told me that there was nobody living in the hills, and that there were no large villages on the island. The place seemed ideal for the influx of an energetic, enterprising group of refugees. The island was about seventy miles long by twelve miles wide and would keep a large number of refugees busy for a long time to come. I couldn't wait to get back and let Mr Van Ban Leeuwin know via the local representative whose dismissive attitude had sent me off on this quest.

"Ewang."

"Yes, Chief."

"We've found it."

"Found what, Chief?"

"The island, Ewang. This is the island for the Vietnamese refugees."

"Does that mean we go home now?"

"This is your new home, Ewang, you're about to become a founding pioneer in the new settlement of Nuova Vietnama. Kneel down and kiss the ground. You're never leaving again."

"But Chief, my wife and child ..."

"I'll send them out here."

"Yes, Chief".

I looked carefully at Ewang as he aquiesced to this suggestion. True to his traditions he wasn't going to argue, but I wanted to try and gauge whether he would run amok or slit my throat while I slept. I decided I had about fifteen seconds before he started plunging daggers into innocent bystanders, and told him he could go home first and discuss with his wife whether they both wanted to return. The glazed look of madness started to recede, and the faint wisps of steam that I imagined I had seen puffing out of his ears evaporated.

# Chapter 14

## Clock on the Tree

I sent Ewang off to buy some coconuts and bananas, issued the chief with some anti-malaria tablets, and declined his offer to stay in the village for a few days. I thought it better not to mention, at this stage, my plan to point the "boat people" in his direction.

We set off during the night, but despite a good breeze our progress was hampered by a strong south-west current. The day's heat was broken up by fierce squalls, in which the rain came across the sea in vertical lines, lasting about five minutes, and was then followed by wind for about fifteen minutes. A thunderstorm was answered by the sound of high explosives over East Timor. A magnificent sunset illuminated Timor, Alor, Liran, Kambing and Wetar, which were all visible at the same time. During the night Ewang wanted to tack off in a different direction. I looked at the compass and found we were going the right way. He, however, had no faith in compasses, preferring to rely on his sense of direction. It made me wonder whether the previous occasions when he had gone the wrong way were errors after all or whether it was magnetic disturbance from the volcanoes. He said he was 'pusing,' 'dizzy,' from my changes of direction. I realised that by not relying on the compass at night he was struggling the whole time to assess which way we were going.

Despite my obvious lack of knowledge and experience he refused to give an opinion on any problem, referring or deferring to my musings. Another inbred cultural difference was his refusal to raise his voice, even when it was required, such as in shouting out depths above the engine noise or bartering across open sea. I recollect constantly shouting, extra loudly as a form of encouragement, "I can't hear you!"

It was almost as maddening as the Indonesian habit of refusing to wake somebody who's asleep.

I watched, and waited for every little shift in the wind and current. No sooner were we making progress than a minor shift of wind, caused by mountains, or the 'moon's passage' tampering with the currents, got me inwardly cursing. Coastal sailing when you're trying to conserve fuel is a frustrating business. The expression "Stuck in the doldrums", now has a new significance for me.

As we reached the top of Alor, the wind misbehaved, and we could do nothing more than head towards the coast. We landed at a nondescript village where the people were completely lacklustre. They showed no interest in anything;

they didn't speak to us or each other. It was probably because they were malnourished to the extent of having distended stomachs, and other debilitating diseases; nearly all of them had infected eyes. They were preparing copra by feebly pecking at some coconuts and laying out the chippings to dry in the sun. I bought ten coconuts, in a transaction so low-key it could have been happening in a supermarket.

A short distance away a mobile trader had also landed and laid out his wares. Sarongs, batteries, hair oil, biscuits - I bought some at five times the price they are in Bali, but I was satisfied because at least they were available - and a battery-powered clock that had been incongruously hung on a tree. It was half an hour slow or 'Indonesian time' as they described it. (In this place they still don't consider themselves 'Indonesian'.) However, it may have been because they didn't know how to alter it.

We moved on down the coast to where a big church stood out against the thatched huts and tropical mountains. The tin sheets on the roof reflected the sun's rays like beams of divine light. A knot of sampans approached with 'armed' men aboard. They held bows and big steel barbed arrows, explaining they were used for 'babi rusa'. As that is a type of deer, I was tempted to ask why they were looking for one out here. We prevented them from coming aboard - why is it that most people only enter somebody's house after being invited in, but seem to regard a boat as common property? The bows were made from bamboo, and the arrows apparently had no flights, perhaps they are fitted just prior to releasing them.

An itinerant trader takes a break, NE Alor Island

The exclusive diet of coconuts and bananas, a change from chilli sauce and white rice cooked in sea water, was having a deleterious effect on my digestive system but in a different way. I felt as though I had been force fed a dozen cans of baked beans. I was reminded of a limerick about getting a boat moving where the last line was 'So they got Carter, the farter to start her', and thought that between the two of us we should have got the *Gin Pahit* moving.

We had decided to head for Kalabahi, the main town of Alor, and try and get some fuel. Ewang was very pleased at this prospect for some reason. Perhaps he had a friend there. Meanwhile the locals were sitting on the pebbly beach watching us. In the evening a church service started, and the singing wafted across the bay.

Later Ewang woke me in an agitated state. A fire had been lit on the bank, the natives were singing raucously, making noises, and worst of all apparently discussing coming aboard. Disgruntled at not being allowed on during the day, they were egging each other on to force their way on now. When a sampan appeared from nowhere, we slammed on the engine and sped away to cries of surprise from the bank.

The next day there was no wind and the sea was like glass. Ewang rigged up an open umbrella at the back of the boat so that the helmsman could keep cool, but we were both very tired. He dozed permanently, either leaning against the engine or lying flat out. We motored to try and get over the reef between Alor and Sika in daylight, but we managed to get the rudder stuck, and then found a sandbank so extensive that we had to backtrack and go round it; then the wind changed; this was followed by a thunderstorm which brought a favourable wind for a short while, and then the current changed to a very powerful south-westerly one so that after two days hard slog we had progressed about half a mile.

We limped westwards, until heading south down the west coast of Alor, and then east up the narrow channel leading to Kalabahi. Like the Bima channel the edges of it rose steeply into a mountain range. A strong wind was blowing up the channel and we took off at high speed, just missing a partly submerged rock near the entrance.

Ewang was visibly happy to be in a town, if the ramshackle collection of leaf-roofed buildings could be called that. My reference book said there were 120,000 people living here, but to the casual observer it looked like one tenth that number. I moved into the Adi Dharma lossman, giving Ewang a chance to relax and chatter with the locals, although this was probably limited as there are reputed to be more than seventy languages on this island, including some of Papuan origin.

The owner of the lossman was a Moslem fundamentalist, and described how they were bracketed with the Communists when there was a purge in the 1960s. The government issued a quota of people to be killed, and he claimed that he had been on this list.

Also in the lossman was an Australian trader called Alan Fenwick specialising in Indonesian ethnic artifacts. He had located some valuable woven mats on the island of Pantar and was in Kalabahi trying to get one of the necessary signatures from an elusive bureaucrat so that he could buy it. Any local article costing more than a certain amount required a patchwork of signatures and a vapour trail of baksheesh before it could officially change hands. Alan said they had originally come from India back in the mists of time. Apart from these imported ones there is a strong local tradition of weaving mats.

He was very enthusiastic about all the things he had seen, and when he heard I'd just been to Wetar, goaded me with stories of the valuable statues to be found there. I had drunk a bottle of John Roben with him, and as it slipped down he became more insistent that the boat would be ideal for ferrying his purchases back to Bali, where he was based. He was on the point of purchasing a collection of megalithic bronze kettle drums decorated with Hindu motifs, but was restrained by their weight and bulk, but if they could be ferried by the *Gin Pahit*... There was also a village only accessible by sea which he had heard wanted to sell some of its artifacts and he was keen for me to take him there. I put myself in his position, and felt a bit of a spoilsport to refuse his request so I told him we'd go wherever he wanted, as long as it was westwards. He couldn't believe his luck, and hurried away to try and sort out his bureaucratic problems, but probably he displayed an iota of impatience and was rewarded with the usual Third World official response: "You'll have to wait until you realise how important I am, and that will probably be a few days." 'Jam kretek' - as they say in Indonesian - 'Rubber time'.

He was in a dilemma but couldn't afford to upset the local officials by displaying the ultimate impatience of leaving and then coming back, so the *Gin Pahit* set sail without him while he chewed his fingernails on the shore.

I decided to give all officials a miss, and as such couldn't hang around too long. And there was no fuel to be bought, which was the main reason for going there.

The boat blended well with the other craft which were all locally built from local materials. The coastal strip was planted with coconut trees, with single-story buildings nestling beneath them. Copra was spread over the beaches, attended by the women and children. In the background, the populated hills were inevitably parched and semi-barren from generations of over-use. The lethargic locals sprawled around the town contemplating these deforested, scorched hills with complacent resignation, and waited patiently for the next volcanic eruption.

We set off on the tide, but the wind inevitably was dead against us. At the mouth of the channel we hit an incredibly strong south going current, and an equally strong north going wind. We tried going north. The boat was pitched around, and even with the engine at full power we made no progress and so turned south. Then the current seemed to change and we tried north again, but hardly had we done that than a new set of conditions prompted us to turn south again, which became a lengthy process as we couldn't get the sail down. Whirlpools and bubbling seas buffeted us around, and in the darkness it became more worrying as we couldn't see where we were heading, and if we had hit something in an area of violent water there was nothing we could have done about it. All the cautions in the pilot book were being demonstrated. I tried to make notes of what the moon was up to so that in quieter moments I could try and make sense of the references to the moon's passage or indeed make my own observations on the relationship between the moon and local conditions. At the first streaks of dawn we made our way towards the south coast of Pantar island, and anchored. Ewang was out of spirits, and I didn't feel much better myself.

A.R. Wallace constantly refers to the same problems, and I felt a kinship with his difficulties a hundred years earlier. In one passage he says:

*We left with a south wind, which suddenly changed to north-east, and induced me to turn again southward in the hopes that this was the commencement of a few days' favourable weather. We sailed on very well in the direction of Teor for about an hour, after which the wind shifted to W.S.W., and we were driven much out of our course, and at nightfall found ourselves in the open sea, and full ten miles to leeward of our destination. My men were now all very much frightened, for if we went on we might be a week at sea in our little open boat, laden almost to the water's edge; or we might drift onto the coast of New Guinea, in which case we should most likely all be murdered. I could not deny these probabilities, and although I showed them that we could not get back to our starting-point with the wind as it was, they insisted upon returning. We accordingly put about, and found that we could lay no nearer Uta than to Teor; however by great good luck, about ten o'clock we hit upon a little coral island, and lay under its lee till morning, when a favourable change of wind brought us back to Uta.*

Again in a similar vein:

*A triangle mast and mat sail carried us on when the wind was favourable, which (as usual) it never was, although, according to the monsoon it ought to have been.*

We eventually arrived at Kampong Nulau, where a local clambered aboard, and said the southern route was best, fifteen minutes later another local appeared and said the north route was easiest. They then both agreed that at such and such a time the current would be doing something. I duly waited and found the current doing exactly the opposite. Local knowledge wasn't proving to be much use. It brought to mind another A.R.Wallace comment:

*I had been promised at this season a calm sea and the wind offshore, but in this case, as in every other, I had been unable to get any reliable information as to the winds and seasons of places distant two or three days' journey.*

In those pre-engine days it was necessary for them to row for long periods when the winds were unfavourable.

Kampong Nulau was one of the villages where Alan had been scouring for artifacts, and no doubt they gave him equally accurate information on the provenance of his 'pre-Colombian' purchases. In the hillside they had constructed an interesting-looking well.

The only course of action was to sail with the current for as long as it lasted, and then anchor using our eccentric looking block of coral to which had been added some scrap metal. It may have been effective, but I didn't see anybody else using a similar contraption.

Suddenly there was both current and wind, the patent anchor was hauled aboard and off we went; this continued until we were nearly at the top of the Pantar Strait, then everything went into reverse. Valuable fuel was used to heave us round the corner, and in doing so we slammed into a coral field and lost all our fishing gear. We anchored again, and Ewang started to display 'John' symptoms - headache, 'not strong' - when I pressed him to question the locals on local conditions. I already knew that it was against local etiquette to ask these sort of questions, and that they wouldn't give a helpful answer, but I felt I had to try anyway.

"They don't understand Indonesian, don't be impatient with them," Ewang said, but it was very difficult not to be as they vacantly said "Yes" to anything addressed to them.

I recognised in myself the irritation coming from extreme tiredness, and tried to dampen it. We either needed more than two people or we should have stopped every few days to regather our strength.

I spotted a motorboat towing a sailing boat, and decided this was a good moment to set off, but it soon became very choppy and the two other boats turned back, Ewang said it was because they thought we were pirates stalking them. Another boat appeared and we followed that for a time before it left us behind. Ahead we could see it taking a wide berth round Pulau Lapan; this coincided with information on the chart in the pilot book and the fact that we had come that way before, but Ewang was sinking fast, and scoffed at it, until we came close and saw the necessity of doing the same thing. We were still off the coral field when darkness came, and with it Ewang's total prostration. To complete the happy picture, some of the underwater turbulence began to manifest itself. Wallace frequently mentions the same thing, and describes the experiences of other people as well:

*We heard a dull roaring sound like a heavy surf behind us. In a short time the roar increased, and we saw a white line of foam coming on, which rapidly passed us without doing any harm, as our boat rose easily over the wave. At short intervals, ten or a dozen others overtook us with great rapidity, and then the sea became perfectly smooth as it was before. I concluded at once that these must be earthquake waves; and on reference to the old voyagers we found that these seas had been long subject to similar phenomena. Dampier encountered them near Mysol, New Guinea, and describes them as follows: 'we found here very strange tides, that ran in streams, making a great sea, and roaring so loud that we could hear them before they came within a mile of us. The sea round about them seemed all broken, and tossed the ship so that she would not answer her helm. These ripplings commonly lasted ten or twelve minutes, and then the sea became as still and smooth as a millpond. We sounded often when in the midst of them, but found no ground, neither could we perceive that they drove us any way. We had in one night several of these tides, that came mostly from the west, and the wind being from that corner we commonly heard them a long time before they came, and sometimes lowered our top sails, thinking it was a gust of wind. They were of great length from north to south, but their breadth not exceeding two hundred yards, and they drove a great pace. For though we had little wind to move us, yet these would soon pass away, and leave the water very smooth, and just before we encountered them we met a great swell, but it did not break.' Sometime afterwards, I learnt that an earthquake had been felt on the coast of Gilolo the very day we had encountered these curious waves.*

Ewang briefly came to life during this disturbance and muttered something about Pulau Marisa which he pronounced Maricha and the best interpretation I could make of it was that he had mistaken Pulau Lapan for Pulau Marisa several miles to the south west. The moon came up at 6.00 pm and went down at midnight, which told me nothing. We got near to Lomblen at 9.30 in the evening and were just off Gulongkeling. The wind was light at this stage but at 10 o'clock it veered to the south and the sail ripped along the stitching. It was no use getting exasperated, so I decided to get some sleep, and deal with the problem when I was feeling fresh.

I woke up early to find Ewang also asleep and the boat drifting. I had told him to wake me if he felt too ill or sleepy to carry on, but of course local etiquette had prevented him from doing this, so the boat was now facing the wrong way and about ten miles back from Mount Gulongkeling and at the same place from where we had started. He explained "I was afraid to wake you as you had just gone to sleep." This was a recurrent problem that Wallace also faced:

*I may mention that I have often found it very difficult to get one Malay servant to wait on another. He will call as loud as he can but will hardly touch, much less shake his comrade. I have frequently had to waken a hard sleeper myself when on a land or sea journey.*

In the following passage he deals with the other difficulty of drifting back in the direction from which one has come.

*At three in the afternoon, when the current turned, we started; but having a head wind made slow progress. At dusk we reached the entrance of the harbour, but an eddy and a gust of wind carried us away and out to sea. After sunset there was a land breeze, and we sailed a little to the south east. It then became calm, and we hung down our anchor forty fathoms, to endeavour to counteract the current; but it was of little avail, and in the morning we found ourselves a good way from shore and just opposite our anchorage of the day before, which we again reached by hard rowing. I gave the men this day to rest and sleep; and the next day we again started at two in the morning with a land breeze. After I had set them to their oars, and given instructions to keep close in shore and on no account to get out to sea, I went below, being rather unwell. At day break I found, to my great astonishment, that we were again far off shore, and was told that the wind had gradually turned more ahead, and had carried us out - none of them having the sense to take down the sail and row in shore, or to call me. As soon as it was day light, we saw that we had drifted back, and were again opposite our former anchorage, and, for the third time, had to row hard to get to it. As we approached the shore, I saw that the current was favourable to us, and we continued down the coast until we were close to the entrance to the lower harbour. Just as we were congratulating ourselves on having at last reached it, a strong south east squall came on, blowing us back, and rendering it impossible to us to enter. Not liking the idea of again returning, I determined on trying to anchor, and succeeded in doing so, in very deep water close to the reefs; but the prevailing winds were such that, should we not hold, we should have no difficulty in going out to sea. By the time the squall had passed, the current had turned against us and we expected to have to wait until four in the afternoon, when we intended to enter the harbour.*

We motored to Kampong Baring in the shadow of Mount Keling where the population was an unlikely mix of Moslems and Catholics. I bought a locally made sarong, some fish and a fruit the size of an apple but with the contents of a pomegranate. A white cockatoo, looking like Edward Lear's depiction of Cockatooca Superba, which they explained was a corruption of 'kaka tua,' meaning older sister, was for sale and its owner said, "It's good at sea". They are highly prized in Bali, but I wasn't confident of it really being a good sailor.

The people were less lethargic but no better at understanding the spoken word. The result was I had to become a coolie-kicker to get my message across. I was forced to karate-chop the sampan boy's hand when he attempted to pull himself on to the boat and upset things on board. Another one who was already on board also needed a karate chop and he spun around as if shot crashing into the sea. The others around the place approved of the action, laughing and repeating the word 'karate.' Before the sampan boy returned to shore I gave him his fee of two razor blades, a cigar and ten rupiahs. One or two of them had been keen to suggest the best time to set sail (the sail having been rudimentarily repaired) and which way, but I was suspicious of their advice in the same way as the driver of an expensive car might be misled by a yokel from whom he had asked the way. However poor, dishevelled and exhausted we might look, there was still a shiny outboard engine at the back of the boat which in local currency was worth more than one million rupiahs and he had just accepted ten rupiahs as his fee. As to John, when Ewang asked, "What happens if this or that takes place?" my stock answer was borrowed from Mrs Thatcher - "There will be no U-turns" - which confused both of them but in the context was appropriate, because it seemed sufficiently graphic and vague to suit their imprecise culture.

# Chapter 15

## *Heading back to Bali*

I wondered what sort of tale Ewang would tell when he got back. He wouldn't be able to say it was too terrible because that would be against his Moslem dignity in suggesting that he had made a poor judgement in coming in the first place. It would be something along the lines that small boats were no good, too much work and that Europeans were difficult. He kept talking about big boats being better. Excessive physical labour goes against the grain of a Moslem, so it was fear of jeopardising his wages that kept him plugging away.

When we came past Lomblen, smoke was pouring out of its volcanic crater, and as we got into the Boling strait, the pilot book referred to north and south tidal slips. I tried to check this with two fishermen who fled into a coral bank; in giving chase we went aground and then we got our makeshift anchor stuck. By the time that was free there was a turbulent water manifestation, and we both went to sleep.

Kalikur, Lomblen Island

Wind and current were completely dominating my life and plans, and when the stream set west with the north wind blowing, I decided to set off to the north coast of Flores instead of going to Larantuka and going round the southern part of Adunara along the Solor Strait. We sailed across the Larantuka Narrows at high speed during the night, hoping not to hit anything; about half way across, and half an hour after the moon went down, a strong north current affected us. By the time the dawn star came up, the Flores hills were well in sight and I wanted to anchor just the other side of the Narrows and observe the tidal streams to try and work out 'the moon's passage' but the only convenient place was too far round. We found a convenient coral bottomed bay from which another boat was just trying to leave but the wind died, and they had to give up their attempt and anchor again. Ewang explained that the boat was probably from Wuring and going to Kalabahi. When I asked him how he knew, as on other similar occasions, he ignored my question as though it was rude. He regarded my map and compass as slightly ridiculous but when I indicated that between the two of them we might be able to go straight to Maumere he affected some respect for them. Contrarily he seemed to get worried when I asked his or other local people's advice. I think he thought my initial declaration of ignorance was false modesty and that he would be on a jolly with a little bit of work thrown in. I had of course hoped that I would pick up some Buginese sailing expertise. So the result was the blind leading the blind but he had changed his attitude about the shallow patches. Previously he hadn't seemed to worry about them but a few bad experiences had taught him that he was as frightened of them as I was. He insisted we change the sail and head further north despite what the compass said. We then changed it back and he went off to sleep. Like John feeling tough not wearing warm clothes and then getting ill, Ewang would wear warm clothes but refused to say he was tired and got ill like that.

Later we set off sailing again, and when we got to Tanjong Babi used the motor to get round it. I picked up a beautiful shell floating in the sea, and once round the point there was enough sea breeze for us to sail slowly. Close to Pulau Babi (the island that no longer exists) turbulent water was spewing out muddy volcanic effluence and I put on the engine to get us through it. A few hours later we arrived at Maumere.

The sampan in which we went ashore sank, but such is the place that it was half expected and my passport and valuables were well wrapped up in polythene. My visa had expired which promised an interesting interview with the police, but it was Sunday and I was told to come back the next day.

The swell was too high in the bay, and we had to go round to Wuring again. I had been about 500 miles, and I gave Tommy a pat, with the request that he hold on for a bit longer.

Ewang was given a suitably warm welcome from his kin while I tended to various physical ailments that were affecting me, painful boils having appeared under my arms, on my side and legs. My toe which I had split open twice in the same spot, was like a tomato, and continued to give me trouble. Wallace also suffered from these boils and I was interested to note his theory for what caused them. The locals told me it was because I didn't eat enough fish.

*I was kept at Passau by an inflammatory eruption, brought on by the constant attacks of acari like harvest bugs, for which the forests of Ceram are famous, and also by the want of nourishing food while in that island. At one time I was covered with severe boils. I had them on my eye, cheek, armpits, elbows, back, thighs, knees, and ankles, so that I was unable to sit or walk, and had great difficulty in finding a side to lie upon without pain. These continued for some weeks, fresh ones coming out as soon as others got well; but good living and sea baths ultimately cured them.*

In my own case I had them almost as badly; the worst one caused my thigh to swell to an enormous size until I attacked it with a blunt razor blade, but it wasn't ready, and I had to wait a few more days before half a pint of pus gushed out leaving a permanent circular scar an inch in diameter.

Three policeman had turned up the day I left Wuring on my way eastwards so I was ready for a grilling when I went to see them. Beforehand however, I set to work trying to repair the sail and bamboo outriggers. It became a Chinese puzzle trying to get the right shape for the three dimensional rigging. However, it did give me an idea. Perhaps the police could be persuaded to give me a letter saying my visa had expired because I was delayed carrying out repairs. The local police and village chief in Wuring were very friendly, even to the point of complimenting the British as a race, but most importantly the fat assistant, who did everything in slow motion, including the rubber stamp, wouldn't write out a paper saying the repairs were responsible for my delay. "That little refinement," he said, "you must get from the Maumere police."

I duly trundled into Maumere police station where I progressed up the ladder of seniority always being asked the same questions until I reached the final plateau, and was then asked a question for the first time, "Have you visited Maumere before?" "Yes, I have." He triumphantly replied, "We knew you were here, you were meant to report to us." A long conversation followed, much of it totally irrelevant. They then summoned Ewang, and questioned him separately, although I could hear what was being said. Ewang was of course as mystified by my trip as anybody else and got them more confused than ever. I winced when they tried to suggest that Dili was my destination, and Ewang, in trying to oblige them seemed to be agreeing with them. At the end of it they would only give me a piece of paper saying when I had called in and when I had left.

Kampong Wuring, Flores

The weather was baking, and I had a headache to match. I bought some supplies, managed to get two of the jerrycans filled with petrol during a thunderstorm and got back to find that nothing at all had been done regarding the repairs. Now that Ewang was back his fellow villagers had no incentive to get things done. Ewang himself, who should have known better, was keen to escort me down to his house so that I could inspect his new baby, and no doubt be prompted into instantly paying him his wages. I duly paid my respects to the new edition to the faith, and suggested that as soon as the repairs were completed I would pay him and be on my way.

I was feeling very much alone. A mass of people were all over the boat, hindering rather than helping, it was pouring with rain, and for the first time in a month the longed-for wind had arrived, which was precisely the wrong moment as it made it impossible to reorganise and repair the sail and rigging that now flapped about out of control. The bamboo outriggers were adrift and half submerged in the water. It combined to provide a strong temptation to try and find the quickest transport back to London.

Eventually a botch job was done on the boat. Ewang was paid, plus a tip which caused him to smile, and I was again reminded of the guide book's remark that 'If they smile you've given too much.'

I left Wuring at 5 o'clock the following morning, and made reasonable progress. Once again I was on my own, and experiencing all the difficulties that are only produced trying to do a two-man job on one's own. As usual it was the rolling and unrolling of the sail that caused the biggest trouble. The approach of a squall had me rushing to get the sail rolled up before it became impossible, and I would then have had to go wherever the wind blew me. In my haste I knocked both kettles into the water, but managed to salvage the old kettle complete with oil lamp reflector serving as a lid.

I anchored but was soon joined by another boat with some persistent deckhands who wanted me to anchor near them. I went over and gave them a bunch of about fifty bananas that had been responsible for some severe indigestion, and pottered away. A couple of fishermen pointed me in the direction of a pleasant bay where I anchored and for some reason felt good. Whatever tomorrow might bring at that particular moment I felt okay. A noiseless sampan sidled alongside containing two obsequious Javanese calling me 'Pak' and explaining they were looking for a village. As the tide went down jagged coral appeared above the surface of the sea, showing me what I had just missed. Ignorance is bliss.

During the night five boats anchored close to me, giving reassurance that this was a popular and safe anchorage. They made a lot of noise, but didn't try and come aboard.

More boils appeared on my arms and legs, causing the most acute discomfort; the slightest pressure, not to mention accidentally knocking them, set off a prolonged, intense pain. My diet, lacking in most minerals and vitamins, was presumably responsible. My supplies of vitamin pills had disappeared along with everything else while the boat was in Bima under John-Robin's care.

I set off early and until 10.00 a.m. the wind was steady from the south east, it then shifted to north-north-west - usually at this time it was west-north-west - and so I had difficulty steering south-west. however, at 2 o'clock it shifted west, and allowed me to go in. The burnt hills were covered in a green sheen from the recent thunderstorms, but I couldn't see whether this was paddy or grass.

At 3.30 p.m. I slammed into some coral, and Tommy chose this moment to start playing up; having extricated myself from it, I limped into Toro Padang. The moon was already up at 5.30 p.m. I slept fitfully until deciding to leave just after midnight when a good breeze had sprung up. The dawn star appeared at 3.45 a.m. and fifteen minutes later the moon went down.

I passed the infamous Reo bay at 2 o'clock in the afternoon, and as there was a good wind changed my plan to anchor on the west side of Toro Besi, where some fishing boats were already anchored, and continued westwards. There was a thunderstorm building over the land, and I was hoping to get far enough westwards to anchor in a good place before the squall struck and blew me out to sea.

There wasn't of course enough time, and cursing myself for not stopping earlier, I now had to sail in as Tommy wasn't working properly. I had knackered myself trying to deal with the sail, and I couldn't just go to sleep for a while. The area towards which I was heading wasn't somewhere from which I could just sail off, I would need to get the engine working or wait for the right winds. I went through a narrow sandy entrance, and immediately was told by some fishermen that I was 'in the wrong place' followed by pointing to another area. Tommy conked out completely at this point, and I was forced to manoeuvre the boat by swimming with flippers on and pushing it. I didn't get very far like this and finally anchored in just about the same spot as I had started. I cleaned the plugs and generally tinkered with the engine to reassure it that it was being cared for, and fortunately it reciprocated by bursting into life at the first tug of the starting cord. I swam ashore, looking by now so integrated that they mistook me for an Indonesian from the Moluccas, and asked me if I was carrying cloves. When I said no, they asked if I had fish. "I'm a tourist," I said, "Oh, a turis," they repeated with a disbelieving air.

However, they were very polite, and uncrowding. It was a Christian village called kampong Piso; the village headman was a very civil person and clearly influenced the other villagers. He must have had some education somewhere because he spotted my boils, which were now worse than ever, and explained it was the lack of 'Vitamin A'. Nobody asked me for anything, and there were no "hey, misters", which may have been because subconsciously I was getting afflicted by 'John's ailment' of being 'setengah mati' - 'half dead' - and clearly was not worth teasing. My thigh felt as though there was a red-hot poker resting on it, the boils under my arms were permanently suppurating, and I was so tired from lack of sleep that I was barely coherent.

I was living on bananas, biscuits, tea and coffee. I also felt, through hallucinatory fatigue, that I was 'eating' as opposed to drinking the water.

Squall-type winds blew through periodically during the night, but the vague pattern I expected along this coast was an offshore breeze from 7.00 until 9.00 in the morning, an onshore breeze from 10.00 in the morning until 2.30 in the afternoon, and after that anything.

In the early morning the restrained knot of spectators saw me off, muttering their surprise that I was going on alone, while a few murmured 'hilang' - 'crazy' - as I wrenched Tommy into life. I got outside the bay and reefs, and at 7.00 a.m. a squall from the sea lasted about an hour making me nervous at times for the sail, but it was replaced by a steady wind from the north-west and I made very good progress. I arrived at Seraya Besar island at 11.30 a.m. but couldn't get the sail down so I continued on to Sabolan Kecil island which I reached at 3.00 p.m. Although I tried repeatedly to get the sail rolled up by using the engine to keep the boat head to wind I was forced eventually to tack back behind Sabolan Besar where in a brief lull in the lee of the island combined with an acrobatic manoeuvre I managed to roll up the sail; but in doing so I gave the boil on my thigh a knock that not only made me vomit with pain but precipitated its demise: it opened out into a crater but without yet discharging the venom inside.

A female friend of mine described how she had a similar boil on her leg when she was sailing in a small open boat with three Thai men. The engine had broken down, and they were forced to swim for several hours to get to the shore. Sheer desperation must have kept her going especially when two of the Thais disappeared beneath the waves.

I was now having to stick to a routine that allowed me to preserve necessary energy. Previously I wouldn't have wasted this valuable wind, and would have made for Gili Lawa Laut just north-east of Komodo.

Heavy thunderclouds over Flores remained as clouds, but dispersed as they came over the sea. I was in a pleasant anchorage close to the shore where I observed some goats apparently drinking the sea water, but presumably they weren't, and I wondered what they did find to drink, or can they survive with just the early morning dew on the scrub?

Habit kept me waking up to check the anchorage, and also during the night my poisoned leg finally discharged half a pint of tomato ketchup. At 3.00 a.m. the boat started bumping on the coral bottom as the tide went out, and I quickly had to gather up the anchor and pole away; one of the springs in the engine necessary for reversing had seized up again, and I had to drape myself over it to prevent it whiplashing out of the water when I applied power. At 3.30 a.m. there was enough wind to sail away, but at 5.00 a.m. the moon went down and with it the wind. A very red dawn with no yellow in it was the prelude to a roasting day.

I passed Komodo and Banta without incident. Both islands were still parched and brown, and very uniniviting. On my way back alone I considered this to be the first of three potentially tricky areas, the second was the Alas Strait, and thirdly the Lombok Trough.

The volcanic island of Sangeang had lava flowing down its side near the top, but lower down were trees and green shoots. A large ship bound for Bima passed too close to me, and prompted me to stop on Sumbawa in a small sandy bay containing a Moslem kampong. After a lot of haggling I acquired four coconuts for a shirt, and a pen which they refused to return after borrowing. The details of this transaction demonstrate my deteriorating mental stamina and judgement. Instead of ploughing on, I should have stopped for a few days and regained my strength. The chief negotiator looked as though he had a dash of Chinese blood in him, and he sported the type of facial hair that is popular with the Chinese and is well described by Wallace:

*One of the chief cock fighters at Dobbo was a Javanese, a sort of master of the ceremonies of the ring, who tied on the spurs and acted as a backer-up of one of the combatants. This man had succeeded by assiduous cultivation in raising a pair of moustaches which were a triumph of art, for they each contained about a dozen hairs more than three inches long and which, being well greased and twisted, were distinctly visible (when not too far off) as a black thread hanging down on each side of his mouth. But the beard to match was the difficulty, for nature had cruelly refused to give him a rudiment of hair on his chin, and the most talented gardener could not do much if he had nothing to cultivate. But true genius triumphs over difficulties. Although there was no hair proper on the chin, there happened to be, rather on one side of it, a small mole or freckle which contained (as such things frequently do) a few stray hairs. These had been made the most of. They had reached four or five inches in length, and formed another black thread dangling from the left angle of the chin. The owner carried this as if it were something remarkable (as it certainly was); he often felt it affectionately, passed it between his fingers, and was evidently extremely proud of his moustaches and beard!*

I decided to move down the coast a little way, and although it was 9 o'clock at night, good visibility owing to a full moon. I sailed off the anchorage, just missing two other boats, out of the bay into the open sea where the fresh wind couldn't match the strong current (perhaps the full moon had something to do with it) and found myself going backwards. I then had to use the engine and travelled a couple of miles up the coast before anchoring again.

In the morning I had to decide whether to go into Bima again to try and get some fuel or risk keeping going with my rapidly diminishing supply. I decided to keep going. Across the top of the Bima channel the chop was bad, and a tug boat emerged towing the 'Harapan' - the boat on which I had gone to Surabaya. Obviously they hadn't been able to get any repairs done there either.

My bamboo outriggers were showing signs of breaking up; they were already covered in a sort of green lichen, and I didn't know whether they were leaking water, and if they did leak and fill up with water whether they would pull the boat down on its side.

Thunderstorms all over the land broke up as they were pushed over the sea. A north west wind made difficult going across Dompo bay, then it died completely leaving an uncomfortable chop, and when it started again it was due west and I had to use more fuel. In the early afternoon, during rain and thunder, I arrived at Kananga moslem village which I had visited before. They clambered about the boat satisfying their curiosity until I asked them if they would like me to enter their houses uninvited and start poking around.

A coffee trading boat was at the village intending to leave at 3 o'clock the following morning for Surabaya. The boat-owner was as vague and uninformative as anybody I had spoken to about 'local conditions'. I was rapidly coming to the conclusion that these people were on a par with the average urban dweller in the West who recognises the name of his neighbouring street, but can't tell you where it is.

The villagers on the other hand were displaying another local trait of giving the answer they thought I wanted to hear. They knew I wanted to go in tandem with the coffee boat, so when I asked in an expectant voice "Is this boat going south to Labuan Haji?" "Oh yes," they chimed together.

"That's a pity," I replied "I'm going north."

"No, no," they chimed together again, "it's really north that his coffee boat is going."

"Wait a minute," I said, "I've made a mistake. It's to the west I'm trying to go."

At which point they gave up, which was a shame, because the coffee boat really was going to the west.

The moon had gone down at 6.45 a.m., and according to the pilot book, strong currents could be expected a week after the full moon. The coffee boat owner was as monosyllabic as could be expected when I attempted to discuss this with him, and his grunts became even more vacant when I told him that my watch kept stopping and that I suspected magnetic disturbance from Tambora volcano. My chart, engraved in 1892, warned of the compass being affected, and after I had twice fed all this information to him, and received neither a grunt nor a nod, I gave up, bought some coconuts and set off for Moyo island, which I reached at 5.30 p.m.

I cleaned out the hole in my thigh which was a perfectly clear cylinder one inch in diameter and three quarters of an inch deep with the muscle at the bottom. The pain, which had receded since it opened, but not gone away, made me feel violent, and I could imagine sailors of old having no trouble being goaded into action while they were thus afflicted; perhaps the British Empire was built on boils. Henry the eighth had a permanent painful karbunkle from a jousting injury, and so boils might have been responsible for his wives and others losing their heads.

At around midnight I saw the coffee boat sailing past, indicating it had left at about 9 o'clock in the evening and not at 3 o'clock in the morning, which had been about the only piece of concrete information that I had been able to get out of the taciturn skipper. In retrospect I haven't the slightest doubt that he thought I was going to hijack his cargo of coffee.

I left soon after he had passed as there was a good breeze. A red and yellow dawn brought a powerful squall at 7 o'clock in the morning which lasted for half an hour, and was followed by a strong wind from the north west. Another one blew across at 9.00 a.m. and then it was sunny. A sail fish with its huge retractable sail out of the water swam along beside me, and likewise a shark had a close look at me with its tail fin appearing occasionally flapping it along.

Several boats had waited to cross the Alas Strait in tandem with the powered boats towing the sailing ones. I arrived at Tanjong Kenanga on Lombok at 2 o'clock in the afternoon, having come from Kampong Kunanga on Sumbawa the previous day, the similarity of names causing the sort of confusion that one would expect.

A stubborn boil on my arm opened up and provided a surge of painful inspiration to get moving again to take my mind off it. I was heading for Ampenan in Lombok where I was going to try and sort out my expired visa, but I suspected I would eventually be directed to the Bali office.

The authorities in Bali take a fairly lenient view on visas, as opposed to most Third World countries, who turn it into a flag-insulting issue.

At 9 o'clock at night I was close inshore and looking for anchorage when I nearly hit several sampans before catching a fishing net round my propeller. This jerked the sampan forward, causing the standing fisherman to be poleaxed into the water. Much to my surprise he was very polite, treating it as his fault, so I paid him more than if he had got aggressive and demanded the moon, which had just risen in the east. A short distance further on I nearly repeated the process and decided to anchor despite the shore being very steep. I asked a fisherman if I was deep enough to stay afloat in low water; he assured me I was, and I duly went off to sleep.

I woke in the morning with the rudder bumping on the seabed, and a row of villagers, perched like theatre-goers in the front row of the stalls, along the edge of the beach, to see what was going to happen. There wasn't of course any question of them offering any help, and I was experienced enough by now not to expect or ask for any. It could be summarized as Moslem villages doing nothing, mixed villages helping a little, and Christian villages being mostly obliging.

# Chapter 16

## The Lombok Trough

There was also the familiar scenario of rocks sticking out of the water in all directions; so I removed the rudder - by now I was an expert at tying the knots and bindings, picked up the anchor and poled myself out. The fisherman who had told me I would still be afloat at low tide sat bemusedly with the rest of them.

Several people were fly-fishing with the skilful use of a kite. By manipulating the string they could dance a fly over the water thirty or forty yards from them. I stopped at a kampong to buy some coconuts. I rejected their first three attempts to sell me 'kelapa muda' - 'young coconuts' - as being old brutes. A young coconut has sweet-tasting water inside and the flesh is soft and palatable, whereas the water in an old coconut is an acquired taste and the flesh difficult to remove and indigestible. Local people usually pour away the water of an old coconut, and use the flesh either for grating and squeezing out the juice for cooking, or drying and selling as copra.

As often happens on an ad hoc trip, it is at the end of it that all the skills and knowledge have been acquired, and one is beginning to settle down, and spend more time on the purpose and less on learning unfamiliar tasks.

At 3.00 p.m. I arrived at Ampenan. The name immediately put me in mind of the nomadic Penan people of central Borneo, but apart from the name there was no other similarity discernible at all. The pilot book described it thus:

*Ampenan is the principal trading centre of Lombok, and is situated close north of the entrance to Kokok Djangkok, the only river which does not dry at its entrance during the south east monsoon. During this season trade by local craft is particularly brisk. Ampenan affords safe anchorage during the south east monsoon and transition periods inside the line of shoals extending south from Medusa reef. During the north west monsoon communication with the shore is often suspended for days in succession, when a blue flag is displayed from the flagstaff.*

In this area the north-west monsoon is from November to March, and the south-east from May to September, with April and October as the transition months. The currents in the area are controlled by the monsoons so that they reverse each other twice a year. As my trip around the area had lasted from August to December, I had gone from south-east, to transition, to north west, and had suffered the predictable confusion. To make it even more confusing there are several places where the currents are not affected by the monsoons, and stay constant. If I had been asked to confirm the above I would have replied that anything can be expected at any time, and I've got a feeling that Wallace would have done the same. In one of his summing-up passages he says:

*It will appear that my experiences of travel in a native prau have not been encouraging. My first crew ran away; two men were lost for a month on a desert island; we were ten times aground on coral reefs; we lost four anchors; the sails were devoured by rats; the small boat was lost astern; we were thirty-eight days on the voyage home, which should not have taken twelve; we were many times short of food and water; we had no compass lamp, owing to there not being a drop of oil in Waigiou when we left; and to crown all, during the whole of our voyages from Goram by Ceram to Waigiou, and from Waigiou to Ternate, occupying in all seventy-eight days, or only twelve days short of three months (all in what was supposed to be the favourable season), we had not one single day of fair wind. We were always close braced up, always struggling against wind, tide, and leeway, and in a vessel that would scarcely sail nearer than eight points from the wind. Every seaman will admit that my first voyage in my own boat was a most unlucky one.*

As it was December it was the north-west monsoon. No boats were anchored, and the surf was very heavy onto the steeply sloping black sand beach. Various sampans approached, having to carefully time the moment at which they put off from the shore because of the violent surf, and I engaged two youths to act as watchmen, and ensure while I went in search of the immigration officer that the anchor didn't drag.

I chartered a bemo with a superior Balinese driver who had worked for seven years with an American timber company on Sumbawa near Kenanga where I had stopped a couple of times, and managed to get petrol. Although it was the middle of the afternoon on a weekday the immigration office was shut, so I went to the chief's house. He was out fishing, no doubt considering that the lack of boats during the north west monsoon was an excuse for him to work part time.

Turtle, Selat Badung

I filled in the time waiting for him, by having some passport photographs made, which I knew he would require by the handful, and eating some tasty food supervised by my driver who organised rambutan and naturally roast Balinese piglet.

When the immigration officer returned, there was loss of face for not being there earlier which made him aggressive and determined to be over-bureaucratic. He wanted three copies of everything brought to his office the following day. There weren't enough 'rubber stamps' from the various authorities, and he wanted to know why there was 'no navy security clearance', and so on and so on.

The return to 'reality' via government bureaucracy after being lulled into another world was always abrupt and tiresome. Each time I hoped, with illogical optimism, that the set of officials would have 'grown up', but of course they merely retired and their places were taken by a new set anxious to prove themselves, show off or just be bloody-minded.

At 7.30 the next morning I arrived to find the second-in-command waiting outside the office, in the same manner that I had waited outside the chief's house, and he scrutinised me carefully as I arrived in my bemo, to see whether I had taken the point.

"You can send your bemo away, this is going to take a long time," was the first thing he said.

As I spoke to my driver the boss arrived and gave me a look that suggested cooperation would be the best course of action, and he disappeared into his office leaving me with his assistant.

After perusing my documents or the lack of them, he said "This is expensive work for the landing officer, it will need 50,000 rupiahs."

"Will he be able to manage with 20,000? " I asked. Not only did I not have much further to go and could afford to use up some of my reserves, but there are moments when it's better to settle than make a point, and it was clearly one of those moments.

"Yes, he could," said the officer, and very quickly a letter was typed up for me to present to the immigration authorities in Bali, leaving him and his chief free to return to their fishing boat.

On my way back to the coast I made a detour to where the larger boats anchor during the north-west monsoon. A 2000-ton petrol tanker was there, and one of the crew was a European. He asked me aboard for lunch, during which he explained that there was a south going current down the Lombok Strait at the moment, but he couldn't give any advice on the best time to leave to cross it.

I returned to the *Gin Pahit* to find everything soaked and the foam inside the vomitorium stinking. Both the boat and myself were on their last legs, and I felt it was a question of one more heave to get myself back to Bali where I could relax for a few days.

I finally settled on 2.30 in the morning as the time to leave. There was a halo round the moon and fractured clouds, but I was still no wiser as to what that meant I should be expecting, and so far I hadn't met any salty old seadogs who could do much better. Because of the advice about the south-going current I steered slightly north. For two or three hours there was just medium chop, but at dawn it suddenly worsened. Porpoises were jumping in front of the boat. I couldn't remember whether this was good luck or bad luck, but either way I took it as a message of 'best of luck".

In the middle of the Strait there was a violent clash of currents, and I had to steer due north, instead of my direction of due west. I needed to pour more fuel into the petrol tank, at the same time as maintaining a safe direction. The vertical waves were breaking and swirling, yet in the distance I could see a ruler line dividing this violent water from complete calm. As dawn came up I saw in the calm water a fleet of Balinese fishing boats heading back to shore, but I couldn't join them because of the direction of the waves and current. If Tommy had faltered now I would have swung round and turned over. All the time I was being forced north into worse water, and yet within visible distance it was okay. I had hit what is known as the 'Ripples' and Wallace describes first the surf at Ampenan and then the Ripples:

*This violent surf is probably in someway dependent on the swell of the great southern ocean, and the violent currents that flow through the Straits of Lombok. These are so uncertain that vessels preparing to anchor in the bay are sometimes suddenly swept away into the Strait, and are not able to get back again for a fortnight.*

*What seamen call the 'Ripples' are also very violent in the Straits, the sea appearing to boil and foam and dance like the rapids below a cataract, vessels are swept about helpless, and small ones are occasionally swamped in the finest weather and under the brightest skies.*

Suddenly a shift in the currents had me into calmer water, but at the same time I noticed a small Balinese fishing boat had got caught up in them, clearly even local craft had a hard time predicting what would happen. In retrospect I should have left at dawn so that I could have seen the water, and avoided steering towards any obviously rough water. As I neared Bali, long undulating waves apparently bouncing off the land regularly swamped the engine but it kept going, and most importantly had kept going at the most crucial moment in the middle of the Ripples.

I arrived at Padang Bai at 9.30 in the morning with a great sense of relief. I baled out the water, had something to eat, and then set sail for Sanur. A huge turtle-like creature with its white shell above the surface of the water, swam next to me for a time.

Presently what is described as the most ugly building in Bali, but was most welcome to me, came into view; it was the concrete edifice called the Bali Beach Hotel. It sticks well above the height of the coconut trees and looks like a solid lump of concrete. Apart from Mount Agung it's the most visible landmark in Bali.

At 2.00 p.m. I swept passed the wreck at the entrance to Sanur harbour, and stopped opposite Made Monoh's house. Luckily he was there, and he swam straight out, clearly relieved to see everything back in one piece. He claimed that John-Robin hadn't been back to Sanur, but was skulking on Lembongan, and occasionally sending over messages. I loaded my gear into a bemo, dropped the engine off at the service centre in Denpasar, and then went on to Legian, and found an empty lossman at a place called Agung Juice Park. I went along to the telephone centre where the usual queue of people were waiting for the single line out of the country. After three hours I gave up and went back.

The following morning I dressed up for my big interview at the Immigrasi. I was told to sit and wait for the standard four hours, affording a glimpse into some of the other cases which were often very similar. Divorced or widowed white women in the rag trade with child or children, emotional, and with a younger Indonesian male in tow were recounting tales of distress. Therapy took place both ways. Frustrated officials got gratification from threatening Westerners with jail, detention, fines or whatever, while the women and children had a valid outlet for some tearful hysteria - "Oh why persecute me?

Everybody is doing it." I did however take a peep at the detention centre when I went to the lavatory, and decided it was a place best avoided if possible. This two way therapy takes a more amusing form on the nudist beaches where European women parade up and down naked, getting titillated from the knowledge that Indonesians are hiding in the bushes watching them.

My turn duly came and I grovelled in the required manner before setting off with a sheaf of forms to the port of Benoa to get everybody from the senior admiral to the man who operated the gate boom to sign, scribble, examine, rubber stamp and lecture, and each time I got referred to the next one I heard in my mind Louis Armstrong singing "What a wonderful world". Finally I returned to the marine section of the Immigrasi and was granted the necessary extension.

The process of unwinding from the trip took a few days, and for the first two nights the sound of the sea nearby made me continually get up half asleep to check for rocks, and the anchor, and ensure that everything was safe. In my dopey state I would then feel that I was deliberately taking a risk by going back to bed; this process repeated itself several times during the night. I was conscious of standing by the open window while all this happened and yet believing I was on the boat.

Agung Juice Park, as its name suggested, specialised in freshly squeezed fruit juices, which, accompanied by some better food than I had had over the last few weeks, soon got me back to normal.

I spent a couple of evenings with various European ecologists discussing some of the flora and fauna I had seen, and hearing rival tales of sea dramas. One frenchman had been in a thirty-ton Bugis boat that had had the mast ripped away by a water spout that passed over them. However, my white manta ray leaping out of the sea and landing with a mighty slap had not been seen by any of them. Roseline Beudels from the Komodo office was knowledgeable and informative in a humorous way about Indonesiana and interested about my description of the Ripples and showed me Wallace's passage about it, which she had marked out anyway as an aide memoire to avoid. Her efforts to provide requested facilities for visiting American scientists had given her much light relief.

Overseas telephone lines continued to evade me, including ones in the Oberoi Hotel. I bumped into Alan Fenwick, the trader from Kalabahi, and I went with him to visit his headquarters in Ubud - a small town up in the hills. He lived with his sister and her boyfriend, 'Cody'; they were in the jewellery business but away visiting Australia at that moment. They lived in converted 'puri' or palace, which was very impressive. Although he had failed to get permission to buy the mats he was after when I met him, there were many other ones hanging up, and their quality was testament to his diligence. An Iban one from the Batang Lupar in Sarawak was of highest-quality workmanship and design. Like many of the Europeans who had lived there for a time, he repeated and seemed to half believe the stories of how certain carvings, especially Kayan ones from Kalimantan, brought bad luck to the extent of plants wilting when they were placed near by. It reminded me of a Woody Allen film scene when he was lying in a hospital bed, and the plant on the cabinet beside him wilted when the nurse produced a large hypodermic syringe.

The prince who owned the converted palace was informed by his witch doctor that Alan's carvings were bringing him bad luck where he was living in Denpasar, so Alan was asked to move them to Sanur, where probably they were spooking Made Monoh and Joh- Robin. Alan also claimed that they were haunting him and to have been relieved when they were moved.

We went for dinner at a place called Murni's, owned by an American and patronised by a cultural cross section. We met a German called Axel who dealt in Balinese paintings, and then were suddenly interrupted by a boisterous American with an East European name, who was known locally as 'Jogja John'. He was a fast-talking, supremely confident New Yorker who endeavoured to get his own way by overwhelming his victim with the intensity of his attention. Nobody could get a word in while he was talking, and in full flow he would be forcing people to agree with him by ridiculing them if they didn't. He used a hilarious mixture of Indonesian and American expressions; nobody had the energy or mental agility to counteract him, and so people preferred to deal with him and keep on the right side of him. He would 'shame' people, by questioning their motives or relationships, into doing what he wanted. As I was a new face, an unknown quantity, I had to be 'recruited' until he could make an assessment, and he did it successfully by making a noisy toast to England, which immediately put me on his side. Alan, however, was a rival trader, and had to be regularly and systematically destroyed. He began by accusing Alan of being a novice and a hanger-on to his sister and 'Cody'. He then started to parody Alan describing a cloth that was hanging on the wall, "You see the whole vibe of this cloth ... and in the design here we have the exhausts of the manta ray ..."

He then got into one of his sustained unbreakable flows where one subject and idea immediately led on to another, and so impressed the sort of people who were making their life up there, "... yes, I can eat potatoes for a week if my mind is working ... that famous impressionist painting Van 'Go', yeh Van 'Go', The Potato Eaters, symbolises the whole business of potato-eating ... on the '73 Everest expedition I prepared potatoes ten different ways, huddled in a valley with my sherpa guide ..."

And on it went until those listening were utterly convinced that he knew all there was to know about potatoes. "Prototypical" was a favourite word of his during these unstoppable flows.

I pottered back to Kuta to change some money, and here I witnessed a familiar Balinese scene take place. An Australian youth on a motorcycle slammed into a push bike with two girls on it; the bicycle was mangled, the girls unhurt, but they kept screaming until they realised the motorcyclist had hit his head and was lying unconscious. A pick-up truck was flagged down, and he was dumped in the back and driven off with the tail gate still down, so if he wasn't dead when he was loaded up, he stood a good chance of being bounced out of the back and finished off.

Throughout the last few days most of my time was taken up trying to organise the simplest but most necessary things - a transfer of some cash from London, and the purchase of an airline ticket. Having got both, I was able to apply for an exit visa for which I was 'fined' 10,000 rupiahs, as an additional slap on the wrist following the recent hassle getting a new entry visa.

Finally all that was left was to bid adieu to Made Monoh, and John-Robin who had made a special effort to get to Sanur. He was trying to be nice, explaining that he had been more or less incommunicado on Lembongan because he was being treated by a witch doctor who specialised in curing mad people. It was an ingenious excuse because I could hardly complain, or give him the hard time that he deserved. He was clearly unbalanced and shouldn't have come along in the first place. He went on to explain that the witch doctor had extracted a lot of evil matter from his body.

"Not by any chance several jerrycans of petrol?" I asked him.

"Oh, I'm sorry about that. My friends were desperate for fuel, and I thought we were going to go back to Bali, and wouldn't need it."

At least he had admitted it, and thereby disarmed the anger I had been preparing for him.

I flew to Singapore, where I sought out my contact at the United Nations High Commission for Refugees and gave her the good news.

"I've found an island for the Vietnamese refugees. It's called Wetar, and it has hot water laid on at Hot Water Harbour."

"Well that's all very interesting," she replied, "because now the Vietnamese refugees are being sent back to Vietnam. Thank you for your gracious desire to help, and I hope you had a wonderful time."

I must admit I was open-mouthed, not because I had wasted my time or because of her attitude, but because the obvious, commonsense policy was being followed.

* 9 7 8 1 8 4 4 2 6 9 0 4 4 *

ND - #0180 - 060826 - C0 - 197/132/13 - PB - 9781844269044 - Gloss Lamination